P9-CRB-943

100 WAYS TO A PERFECT EQUINE PARTNERSHIP

Susan McBane

David and Charles

A DAVID & CHARLES BOOK

David & Charles is an F+W
Publications Inc. company
4700 East Galbraith Road
Cincinnati, OH 45236

First published in the UK in 2007

A catalogue record for this book is available from the British Library.

ISBN-13: 978-0-7153-2485-1 hardback
ISBN-10: 0-7153-2485-3 hardback

Printed in Singapore by KHL Printing Co Ltd
for David & Charles
Brunel House Newton Abbot Devon

Commissioning Editor Jane Trollope
Editor Jennifer Proverbs
Editorial Assistant Emily Rae
Designer Jodie Lystor
Production Controller Beverley Richardson

Visit our website at www.davidandcharles.co.uk

David & Charles books are available from all good bookshops; alternatively you can contact our Orderline on 0870 9908222 or write to us at FREEPOST EX2 110, D&C Direct, Newton Abbot, TQ12 4ZZ (no stamp required UK only); US customers call 800-289-0963 and Canadian customers call 800-840-5220.

Contents

Introduction

Forging a brilliant partnership with your horse is a most rewarding thing to do. Whether you have had your horse for a long time but have always felt that there was something missing, or whether you are new to each other and, perhaps, one or other of you has had problems in horse-human relationships, getting it right at last is often a turning point in both your lives. This book is meant to help you with many aspects of that process, and I sincerely hope that it will do so.

It is the last one in a series of five books devised by David & Charles to suggest to readers 100 ways to improve certain aspects of horse ownership. The other four are listed in Further Reading on page 151. Some aspects have unavoidably occurred in this book as well, but readers will find references in the text to the others for fuller information. All the books are available through good libraries, but you may prefer to build up your own full set of all five. Good bookshops can get them for you, and they are available from the Equestrian Book Society. I have very much enjoyed writing them, and I do hope that you will gain a lot of pleasure and knowledge from them.

The Five Freedoms

So what constitutes an acceptable code of practice for managing equines, and where, and how, can we find out about it?

The 'Five Freedoms' is a concept probably familiar to many people dealing with animals, not only horses. The 'freedoms' apply to domestic and captive animals, and constitute a code of practice for the people looking after them, to help them assess whether their management regime does in fact adequately meet the needs of the animals in their care. Some would say that if the animals' needs are not being met, they are actually being abused. The factors covered are all those likely to influence the welfare of the animals. They are:

1 **Freedom from thirst, hunger and malnutrition** – by providing access to fresh water, and a diet to maintain your horse's full health and vigour.
2 **Freedom from physical and thermal discomfort** – by providing a suitable environment, including shelter and a comfortable resting area.
3 **Freedom from pain, injury and disease** – by prevention or rapid diagnosis and treatment.
4 **Freedom to express most patterns of normal behaviour** – by providing sufficient space, proper facilities and company of the animal's own kind.
5 **Freedom from fear and distress** – by ensuring conditions that avoid mental suffering for the animal.

These five points constitute a perfectly reasonable, basic 'duty of care' for anyone responsible for looking after animals, and it is their responsibility (and, in UK law at least, the legal owner's, even if the caring part is delegated to someone else) to implement a suitable management regime for the type of animal involved. Readers of a book like this probably know of many horses and ponies (not to mention other kinds of animal) in all sorts of establishments, where the way they are looked after falls well short of the standards set out in the Five Freedoms.

To implement a correctly and humanely based management regime, you need knowledge and

Freedom from physical and thermal discomfort: This means providing stabling and grazing that is safe and will not cause him injury or sickness, and which provides shelter from extremes of cold *and* heat, from insects and from aggressive animals. The horse needs somewhere safe and comfortable to rest in peace. We must also give careful thought to the comfortable fit and humane use of tack and clothing (too much of the latter is just as bad as too little). In addition, we must not work or keep horses in ways that cause them discomfort or distress.

understanding, plus empathy, or a 'feel' for horses. Nowadays there are many good books available to help you acquire the necessary knowledge, besides videos, DVDs, CDs, clinics and courses, and there are some good riding schools. It is of paramount importance that owners increase their knowledge as much as they possibly can, and gradually learn to use their own judgement and sensitivity. Asking other horse owners can widen your knowledge of opinions, but the advice you receive may not be accurate or suitable. It is best to rely on specialist experts such as your veterinary surgeon, a good farrier, the nutritionists on the helpline of the company whose feeds you use, a teacher who seems to really have the interests of your horse at heart, and so on.

Let us briefly consider the Five Freedoms as they relate to horses, who evolved as running, grazing, social herd animals, free to find food, water and shelter, free to socialize and play with their friends, and to gallop away from any suspected danger – whether hostile equines, or some other predator – to which they are always alert and instantly reactive. They evolved to thrive on a very varied diet of vegetation, mainly grasses, of fairly low feeding value but constantly available.

Freedom from thirst, hunger and malnutrition: This freedom is crucial to health and contentment. One of the safest ways to feed most horses is to give them fairly constant supplies of suitable forage (hay, haylage, short-chopped forages or grazing) and clean water, plus maybe a vitamin and mineral supplement. It is essential to leave the horse ample supplies to last him for several hours, such as overnight or when his carer is at work. This is often overlooked, and the horse left for long periods without food and clean water.

Freedom from pain, injury and disease: This means effective preventive management, careful work and being willing to call in veterinary attention quickly when accidents or illness occur.

Freedom to express most patterns of normal behaviour: This might include eating grass and drinking; meandering around; mutual grooming and socializing with friends; rolling, lying flat out to sleep properly; bucking, kicking or galloping; and plenty more. This means that horses should be turned out so they are free, outdoors or under cover, with their companions, for some hours, and normally every day.

Freedom from fear and distress: Horses can be frightened by all manner of things: by rough, loud, cruel people; by traffic; by any situation that causes their adrenalin to flow; by being forcibly restrained, beaten up, forced into vehicles or ridden harshly; by being harassed by dogs or other animals; and by many other occurrences and situations.

Distress (mental suffering) is caused by a lack of the bare necessities of life (food, water, shelter, freedom and company), by neglected teeth, sore feet, uncomfortable tack and clothing, over-confinement, bad air conditions, untreated injuries or diseases, and many other eventualities.

By paying conscientious, knowledgeable attention to the Five Freedoms, not only can we recognize when horses and ponies anywhere, and in whatever ownership, are being deprived of them, but we can also ensure that our own horses do not fall into that category.

Your relationship with your horse

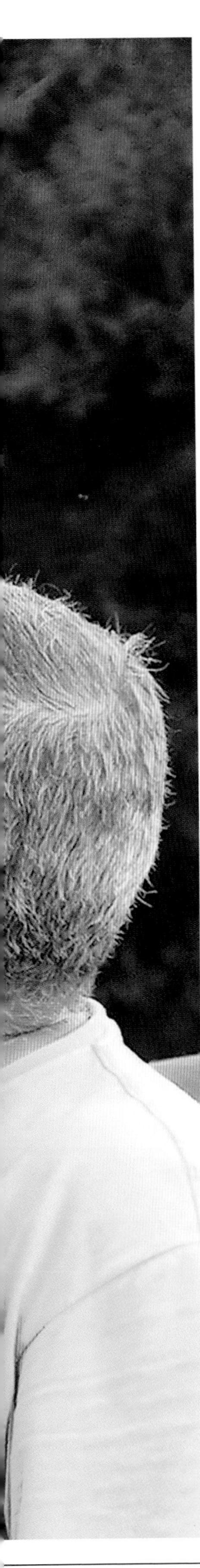

Creating the relationship

This book is all about forging a strong and mutually beneficial relationship with your horse, about bonding with him, about creating a trusting partnership – in short, you want a true equine friend and your horse wants a human he can trust and rely on.

Horses basically want to be comfortable and to feel safe and secure. In order to forge a close relationship we must make the horse feel that way in the environment we provide or create for him, and, crucially, in our company. He must feel as content with us as he does with trusted field-mates and friends, not always choosing them above us, as do many horses.

Some signs of a good relationship are that your horse calls to you and to no other human, leaves his friends and comes to you knowing that you don't carry titbits, is quite willing to be with, and to work with you alone, will let you do unpleasant but necessary things to him, comes and tries to tell you if there is a problem, remains lying down when you enter his stable, does things for you he obviously does not want to do, does not try to harm you, and does more than merely tolerate you.

Horses need to feel that they belong with you and rely on you for their needs and wants. I firmly believe, too, that they need a kind of leadership/guidance/support/protection – call it what you will – so that they know where they stand, as in a herd. Most horses are not aggressive with each other, but they are not particularly kind either. Horse play and assertiveness *are* rough and can hurt, and a 'superior' horse will allow only special friends and relations to behave towards him in ways he would not tolerate from any others. Less favoured herd members get put, or are sensible enough to stay, in their place.

What do *you* want out of this relationship? You'll want a horse who seems glad to see you and to be with you, to do things with you, and who trusts you. He won't overstep the line, will try for you even when he is concerned about something, and will not intentionally harm you.

When things get really good between you, he will put you in a different category from other people, pay you a lot of attention when you are around, and try to tell you when he has a problem. He will prefer to be cared for and ridden by you, although accepting others, and he'll show relief and become calm when you appear on the scene of trouble.

Many of the ways in which horses behave on the ground and under saddle are the result of training and learning, whether this is intentional on your part or not; but with a horse you know well and whose inclinations you can sense, you will know whether his behaviour stems from the habit of training, or from an inclination of will.

This first section discusses some of the ways in which you can lay the foundation of a close relationship with your horse.

1 Create the feel-good factor

Because basically horses just want to feel comfortable, safe and secure, we can deal with these three elements together and call them the 'feel-good factor'. Of course life for anyone, human or animal, is not all sunshine and light – far from it, very often – but we should try to make it as close to that state as possible for our horses if they are to feel good and associate us with an 'everything's all right now' attitude.

Why is this so important?

All 'higher' animals – and not only mammals such as horses and people – feel pain, discomfort, heat and cold. They also feel emotions such as excitement, anxiety, frustration, depression, contentment and fear, and many others. Basically horses like a mainly quiet life, with some periods of enjoyable physical sensations such as grooming with a friend, or feeling fit and well and galloping like the wind, and good emotions rather than bad ones.

Because the horse is a prey animal, it has a particular concern for its own comfort, safety and security, maybe more so than a predatory animal. Domestic horses and ponies retain their species natural, instinctive wariness, and it doesn't take much to arouse their adrenalin, and trigger their fright, flight or fight response. Anything stressful or frustrating can cause this reaction, which is why so many horses kept in conventional domestic conditions (individual stables and small paddocks with frequently fluctuating and over-crowded populations) show behavioural abnormalities, not just the more familiar 'stable vices'. Anything frightening will cause a lightning quick reaction because horses are biologically programmed by evolution to flee if possible and fight if not.

Regular exposure to these situations does not make for calm, psychologically stable horses who feel comfortable, safe and secure and, therefore, content.

What can I do?

It can be difficult to go along with the following advice if you keep your horse at livery and/or work or study full time, but these are two of the best ways to create the feel-good factor as part of the relationship you are aiming for:

1. Be with your horse as much as you possibly can.
2. Make every effort to be the one who handles and reassures him during procedures that might be uncomfortable or even a bit painful, such as having his feet and teeth seen to, or receiving veterinary attention (for example, having a wound cleaned, stitched and dressed).

Many people who own horses do not take their holidays for weeks at a time, but save up their leave days or 'flexitime' (flexible working hours) to take off perhaps just half a day so they can be with their horse, or be at the stables at a convenient time midweek to ride or attend to his comfort, and so on. Shift workers are often in a better position to do this, especially during the short days of winter, than those who work a rigid 9am-to-5pm, Monday-to-Friday job. (If you are in that position, see Further Reading for other books that should help you a great deal in this.) To be realistic, you can hardly expect to be a VIP in your horse's estimation if you only see him at weekends, or spend your midweek time with him on edge and rushing to get the chores done.

Is there anything else I can do?

Whenever you are with your horse, pay great attention to your demeanour and his comfort. Horses prefer quiet, confident people who increase their comfort and do nothing to hurt or aggravate them.

As soon as you arrive at the yard or field, go straight to your horse (he'll probably know you've arrived because of his superb sense of hearing, and he won't appreciate your talking to other people or animals first – honestly!). Greet him by letting him sniff you, which helps him confirm your identity and tells him about your physical and emotional state – so think happy and calm. Stroke, don't pat, him low on the neck and withers: stroking and rubbing in this area, which is mainly where horses mutual groom each other, which they do quite firmly, has been shown to lower the heart rate and help him relax.

Immediately check that he seems comfortable: that his rug, if worn, is not pulling on his shoulders and pressing on his withers (if it is, loosen it immediately); that his headcollar, if worn, is comfortable; that he has clean water and fibrous forage available (unless you have asked someone to bring him in so he stands in for a short time before you work him); and that any boots, wound dressings, fly hoods and so on are in place, clean and comfortable.

Checking the state of his box, yard or paddock tells you a lot about his behaviour in the hours before your arrival. Also, check his facial expression, body language and general demeanour to discover how he feels. When dealing with him, do so considerately and gently, but at the same time confidently so that he, too, feels confidence in you. Verbally reassuring him adds to his acceptance of uncomfortable procedures and treatments. Horses definitely understand, and accept that everything is really all right even though the circumstances affecting them at that particular moment might seem to be unpleasant, and gaining their trust in such a situation is truly a feather in your cap.

2 Understand your horse's world

Probably one of the biggest mistakes we make as horse owners – and it's an understandable one to make – is to assume that our horses perceive and experience the world as we do. But they don't. As mammals, we are both very closely related, and all mammals have the same basic equipment – but the horse's evolution and senses give him a quite different reality from ours.

How the horse evolved

Many animals live by eating other animals, and many live by eating life of a different sort – vegetation. Although we humans eat both, we function mainly as the former, as go-getting predators, whereas horses are defensive prey animals who want to be left in peace and to eat grass. They are most active at dawn and dusk, whilst we are diurnal. We clearly have very different outlooks on life.

Horses' minds and bodies are brilliantly designed to be classic outdoor, running, grazing plains animals. They have:

- an adaptable, wary mind that is quick to learn and that never forgets;
- a brain that can go from fast asleep to wide awake and running within two or three seconds;
- the ability to accelerate to a top speed of around 40mph in a similar timescale;
- long legs for running, with energy-conserving elastic tendons and lightweight, easy-to-move lower legs that are finished off with hard but sensitive hooves;
- a kick that can kill or seriously disable predators or rivals;
- a bite that can do the same when the horse is cornered or fighting;
- capacious lungs for the exchange of oxygen and carbon dioxide;
- a super-efficient heart and circulatory system for pumping blood around this speed machine to deliver fuel and oxygen and remove waste;
- back-up supplies of red blood cells to maintain speed and stamina over long distances;
- muscles that can even work without oxygen when the chips are down and the horse is fleeing for its life;
- a long head and neck to enable the mouth to reach the ground to eat and drink (refuel);
- large, strong teeth and jaws to grind up tough food during most of the horse's waking hours;
- the ability to rest standing up, ever ready to run, due to a locking mechanism in the legs;
- superb senses of hearing, and particularly smelling, for the detection and recognition of predators and other animals;
- almost all-round vision geared to both detecting nearby movement and scanning the horizon.

This is a formidable survivor for the environment in which it evolved, but a quick run down the list shows how inappropriate our view and our management of one of nature's specialist animals often is.

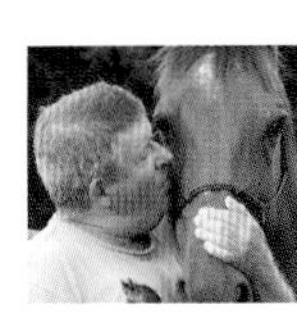

What his senses tell him

The horse's sense of touch is very highly developed. He can feel the lightest touch on his coat and is probably less able to stand pain and discomfort than we are. His sense of taste again is similar to ours, and geared to distinguishing between sweet, bitter, salt and sour. Where his senses diverge more from ours are in his hearing, his sense of smell and especially his vision.

Hearing: Horses have a wider hearing range than humans, and can hear higher-pitched sounds. They can pick them up more efficiently because of the funnel-shaped outer ear, which gathers in the sound waves, each ear moving independently in a 180-degree semi-circle to do so.

Smell: Horses' sense of smell is far superior to ours, being almost equal to that of the dog. Smells can apparently be detected a mile away if the wind is in the right direction, and horses are capable of following an old or fresh scent trail on the ground or in the air. They use smell to identify not only other animals, whether present or having just passed through, but their physical and emotional states, as well.

Vision: The horse's eyesight would probably frighten us all to death! Because their eyes are set at the side of their head, horses can see almost all around them, receiving (and being able to assess) a different picture from each eye and having an overlap area in front when both eyes are directed on the same view. They also have a blind area immediately in front of their head in an upward direction. They see reds, oranges, blues and purples well, but probably not yellows and greens.

The most startling research discoveries about equine vision include the following:

- Their field of vision, which is a horizontal strip almost all around them compared with our frontal, circular field of vision.
- Their indistinct vision, which is comparable to the standard we perceive 'out of the corner' of our eyes. They have no sharp, clear area of vision at all.
- They see best in dim light and poorly in bright light. Horses who have been taught to control their own lighting in an enclosed barn choose dim light all the time.
- They can barely focus at all with their lenses and for the best view must manoeuvre their head position to bring objects on to a 'visual streak' across the lower back of the eye (on to the retina).

The meaning of it all

Firstly, as a prey animal, the horse is 'hard wired' to run first and think later. We can overcome this tendency by a calm, strong and empathetic attitude in management and training. The horse is not stupid or scatter-brained – he is a normal prey animal, and that is not his fault.

Secondly, we must realize that he is picking up, and may act upon, a lot more messages from the world than we ever will. His heightened hearing and ability to smell must make him think we are either half asleep or remarkably stupid because we clearly miss so much! Horses rely much more on these senses, because ...

Thirdly, their vision is geared to detecting movement and shape, not clear, sharp, colourful detail. Only primates and birds can do that. This is why horses appear to see better in the dark than we do, but also why they cannot assess strange objects and may shy and jink about. It becomes clear that we must not restrict their head position when jumping or on rough ground. Making a horse go with his head rigidly fixed or his face behind or even on the vertical effectively blinds him to what's ahead and cannot be condoned, on welfare grounds, surely?

Finally, the key to safe, rewarding relationships lies in establishing two-way communication and trust. Horses need to know that if they trust us nothing awful will happen – and what a responsibility that is! We must also trust and use, and permit him to use, his heightened abilities to assess and cope with our mutual environment.

In short, a successful relationship between horse and human is a tall order for both parties.

3 Listen to your instinct and conscience

Most people have a personal code of ethics by which they live. An excellent 'rule of living', given good psychological health and whatever your culture, is 'Treat others as you would like them to treat you'. Most of us want to be treated humanely and with good manners, which simply means having consideration for the other person. As a horse owner, you can apply the same ethics to your horse.

How does this relate to my horse?

It means that you should never let anyone do anything to your horse that your instinct or conscience tells you is wrong for him, and that you should never do anything like that to him yourself. Of course, your horse is a horse and not a human, and this brings us back to the importance of acquiring as much knowledge as you can about caring for him, and riding him. Once you have managed to do this, at even a basic level (which doesn't take long), you can then more usefully rely on the realms of instinct and conscience.

Often we may not be in a position to control our horse's management entirely because of, say, conditions at our livery yard. But at some point the knowledgeable, sensitive owner starts to get that uncomfortable feeling of being nagged to do something about it.

What can I do?

Pay attention to that feeling above all else. Don't brush it aside. Act on it.

- If you have a trainer who rides your horse harshly (which is different from the firm handling sometimes needed to establish reasonable discipline), says he 'needs a good hiding' and expects you to go along with this philosophy, stop the lesson, pay in full, and don't book that trainer any more.
- If your livery yard restricts turnout unreasonably (for example providing none, or only an hour a day), arrange some elsewhere, possibly whilst you are looking for another yard. The yard proprietor may have what he or she calls 'a good reason', but the fact is that most horses need significant freedom on most days with compatible companions, maybe on a surfaced enclosure if necessary.
- If anyone treating your horse gets loud or rough as opposed to tactfully firm, tell them about it and, if necessary, stop the procedure at once; there will always be someone else who can do the job more professionally.
- If your livery yard requires you to buy your supplies from them, and will not buy in good quality products, point out that this is not acceptable from a welfare viewpoint, and insist on buying your own. Again, you may need to find another yard.

There is generally a way round most problems, with a little thought.

4 Spend 'quiet time' with your horse

The majority of horse owners are not able to spend most of their time with their horse. They may work, have a business or family, elderly relatives or other time-consuming responsibilities, all of which take time away from their equestrian interests. It's as much as many people can do to get the chores done and ride, let alone spend other time with their horse; nevertheless, the rewards of 'quiet time' are tremendous.

What is the value of quiet time?

Spending time just in companionship with your horse may give you a completely different view of him, his outlook and his life, his likes and dislikes, which his real horse friends are, and his attitude to you.

Horses in nature, including those turned out with sociable friends in good conditions for long periods, are basically quiet, peaceful animals. Of course, they like to indulge in horseplay and cavort around, and maybe 'test the water' regarding relationships and status, but they are not normally violent unless they have good reason.

Joining in this innate inclination of horses – to be peaceful and companionable – will certainly improve your relationship, and your partnership or bond, with your own horse or horses. It is quite reasonable to suppose that horses often consider us, their owners, to be anti-social, in their terms, if all we ever do is busy ourselves as soon as we arrive at the yard or field, never standing still, chatting most of the time to other humans, rushing about doing 'chores', only finding the time to give the horse a quick grooming and exercise session – then more chores and we're gone. Rushing around, physically and mentally, is not peaceful, neither is it companionable, and horses know this.

What can I do?

Visit your horse as often as you reasonably can so that you become a frequent feature in his life. Unless he is desperately short of healthily taxing exercise, or needs to be kept athletically fit for his job, you don't have to ride him every time you visit. Try walking him out in hand instead, grazing on any spare patch of grass you can find: put his rugs on if it is cold, walk and stand with him, stroke him and watch him, showing an interest in what he is eating or looking at. You can also sit and read in his box or field, stand with him when drinking your coffee, and generally include him in your life more as a friend and not so much as a responsibility and a conveyance.

I'm sure you'll come to love this different aspect of your relationship, and your bond will grow accordingly.

5 Establish a reasonable routine

We hear a lot about strict stable routine, and certainly there is something to be said for doing things at the same time every day – but we all know of instances when it just isn't possible, show days being one example and 'treatment' visits from the vet or farrier another. Horses have a kind of relaxed routine of their own, but our idea of routine is largely for our benefit. With a bit of forethought, horses can benefit, too.

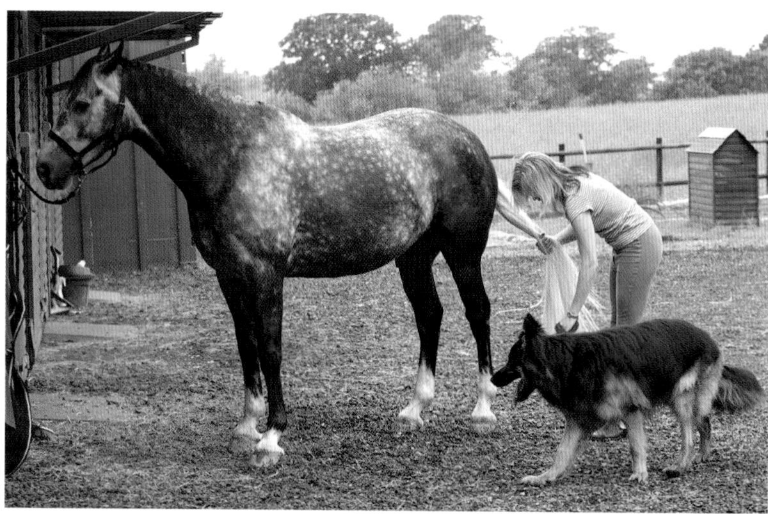

The pros and cons of routine

Provided that the people arranging the routine are good horse managers and know their job, whether formal or informal, a routine is one way of ensuring that everything that needs to be done for horses on a daily basis gets done at an appropriate time. It enables we humans to run our lives by the clock, if we have to, and to fit in all our tasks with the comforting knowledge that we are on schedule and everything will get done.

On the downside is the fact that strict routines are extremely tying, and it can be really stressful to know, for instance, that you are stuck in traffic and can't get to the yard for feeding time, when all the other horses will be fed. Mobile phones are useful, of course, as long as there is someone you can ring!

What can I do?

Situations on different yards, whether your own or a livery yard, can vary a good deal. Basically, in yards where there seems to be no strict or actual routine, individual horses appear to be quite content provided they always have their basic needs in place: food, water, company, shelter and somewhere to kick up their heels every day. In this situation, horses do not seem to bother much if their various 'maintenance tasks' are not performed right on time.

Having the knowledge that things will be done around a certain time goes a long way towards removing the anxiety that can be caused by hunger, thirst, over-confinement, exposure and lack of company.

You could set your watch by them ...

Horses do 'know the time'. A friend and I once kept our horses at a yard where the owners (farmers) operated a very free-and-easy system for their own half-dozen horses. These were allowed to wander more or less wherever they wanted around fields and farmyard, and during the several months that we were at the yard over summer, autumn and winter, they would remarkably all turn up at the stables at 4pm to come in, eat, drink and rest for the night. This was, of course, despite the fact that the days were shortening all the time, so they weren't using the sun's position as a guideline.

6 Let him know what's coming next

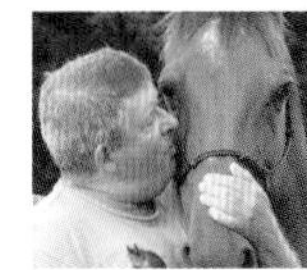

So how can you do that – let him know what you are planning to do? You can't exactly explain to him in plain English that you are just popping off to the feed room to get his tea, even though it's half an hour early. Nevertheless, one big advantage, if we use it right, is that horses form habits and associations extremely quickly and easily, for better and for worse. So how can we take advantage of this without making ourselves a slave to our own routine?

Forming a habit

Most behavioural scientists tell us that horses operate mainly by instinct, 'hard-wiring' from their evolution and habit. Not everyone agrees, scientist or not, but let's consider this and take picking out feet as an example of the formation of a habit.

If you take a young horse and teach him to have his feet picked out, you and he will find the whole four-feet process easier if you start with the same foot and go round the other three in the same order each time. He will see you carrying the hoofpick, perhaps, and standing by the first leg to be lifted. He will shift his weight off it or even lift it, and before you arrive at the next one a well-habituated horse will already have it hovering in the air.

As he lifts each foot, you can say 'up' so that he comes to associate that particular sound with lifting a foot; then every time that he hears you say 'up', he will pick up whichever foot you are standing by, and this very quickly becomes a well-established habit. Furthermore, not only will your horse pick up his feet readily, but also, being able to anticipate where you are going around him and what you are (probably) going to ask for, gives him a sense of security because this is harmless, familiar ground.

But what if I want him to do something different?

All you have to do is stand by whichever foot you want, say 'up', or even just bend and touch the leg, and the foot will almost certainly come up in a well-handled horse who trusts you. He is, in fact, responding to where you are standing, the instruction 'up' and your body posture (bending and touching the leg), not exclusively to the order in which you normally pick up the feet.

Responding to regular, very similar sounds and postures has become his habit. A horse new to you may be used to doing all this in a different order and to different sounds and positions, but if you are consistent he will soon form a new habit, and you won't have any trouble.

7 Accept your horse's limitations

As we all know, there is no such thing as the perfect horse or pony. Although some come extremely close to it and are known as 'very hard to fault', there is no such thing as perfect conformation. Less-than-perfect behaviour is also becoming much more common, and quirks of temperament may be quite irritating to some people. On the whole, most horses will come with physical or behavioural imperfections.

His physical limitations

If your horse were nearly perfect, he would have cost a very great deal of money and would probably be classed as international team standard. By contrast there are some really odd-shaped horses winning races and doing well in show-jumping and cross-country competitions, not to mention hunting brilliantly. For example, there was a Czechoslovakian steeplechaser some years ago who was a brilliant performer despite having a significantly deformed foot and leg.

Often the body can compensate for its own minor deficiencies by adapting the way it moves, and this may enable the horse to cope at whatever level he finds easy. Usually, horses with conformational defects function quite well until they come under just a bit too much physical stress; then they experience discomfort, anxiety and even pain, which is shown up by performance difficulties such as moving badly, refusing fences, and 'bad' or rather defensive (actually protective) behaviour under saddle. Clearly the caring owner will not push the horse beyond what he finds easy, and will be willing to take expert advice on the matter.

Many conformational defects can be helped by correct schooling to strengthen the appropriate muscles and improve posture, which will help the horse to cope; also perhaps by skilled farriery and physiotherapy.

With expert advice, you can always restrict your activities, whether or not you compete, to those the horse is good at and can do well within himself, avoiding the others. From a relationship viewpoint, it is no good persisting with something that distresses your horse: this is a sure way to destroy his trust and co-operation.

Physical limitations caused by disease, injury or allergy – such as osteoarthritis, tendon or ligament weakness or poor lung function, for example – may also leave their mark and decrease the horse's physical capabilities. The solution is often a case of the horse being given less demanding work, plus therapeutic and management techniques to minimize the effects of his problems.

Behavioural limitations

Not all horses have the perfect temperament for, or attitude to their work. Temperament is something the horse is born with, and nothing will change it, but correct training and an approach appropriate to his temperament can still produce excellent results. It is also becoming increasingly common for a horse to be subjected to poor handling and management, which leads to his becoming a so-called 'problem horse'; however, remedial training is now developing into a field in its own right and is readily available in many areas, at least in the UK. Some horses have been transformed in attitude and behaviour through the use of such methods.

Sometimes, all that is needed for such a miraculous turnaround is for a horse and owner to 'gel', or get on really well with each other, and at times it does seem as if Fate has had a hand in drawing certain combinations together; however, if your relationship does not come within that realm, you can still form a close bond with your horse, even if this means compromising and being content with the qualities (and the shortcomings) that you each have. This happens all the time. Ideally you just seem to understand each other, and although you may have your differences, generally speaking you form a partnership that is usually mutually co-operative.

Remember that you can learn more by meeting a 'difficult' horse halfway. This can take time – but it is immensely rewarding when a horse that you thought you would never get on with clearly starts to regard you as his or her partner, goes like silk for you and welcomes you into his space, and obviously feels as though all is right with his world when you are around.

Changing your goals

With horses of this kind, you may need to change your ideas of why you wanted a horse, of what you intended to do with him, and of the kind of relationship you expected. You may find that things are not working out as you planned, expected or wanted, but that even so, you are getting really fond of the horse – and then you should listen to your heart as well as your head because it could be that, despite what you see as limitations, you were meant to be together and could achieve wonderful things with each other that delight both of you: and that's really all that matters.

In my own experience I can relate my partnership with a hot, opinionated mare who had been charging off with me for months and whom I never thought I should be able to manage. But after months of giving her my heart and soul, she finally accepted them and would then do anything for me; finally being able to enjoy an easy, rocking-horse canter on her down a particularly tempting, dead-straight bridleway gave me the feeling of truly heaven-sent achievement every time I did it.

If you really love your horse, tact and compromise will often bring rewards that are beyond price.

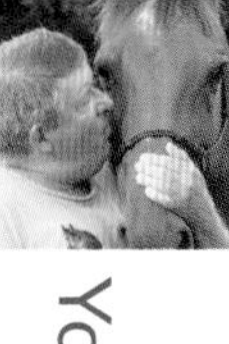

8 Treat your horse as the most important

Here again we have the hierarchy/no hierarchy argument. Some say that horses do not have a hierarchy or pecking order, others insist that they do. Some think that they are not competitive as regards status; others believe just as strongly that they are. I have read many scientifically based arguments and many lay opinions, and have discussed the issue with a great many people – and I am coming down in the middle!

Think like a horse...

We've heard that before and, of course, it is much easier said than done. Humans are often very competitive, and status is important to many of us: in business, being the favourite of the departmental manager or the company chairman is a sure sign of status.

In a field of horses, things are a little different, but there are still indications that some defer to others in certain areas of life – such as grazing, favoured company, shelter, watering order and so on – and of others who appear to be given the first pick of certain, though not necessarily all, desirable facilities. There is also often one unfortunate who seems to be at the bottom of the heap for everything and bears the brunt of others' frustrations, despite his innocence. If this is your horse, you'll naturally be concerned for him.

What can I do?

You may think that there is nothing you can do about relationship dynamics within a herd. However, I recall how an academically highly qualified contributor once reported that treating a horse as 'number one' in his group can raise his status in the eyes of the others. Needless to say, other highly qualified behavioural scientists have denied this assertion because they maintain that 'horses don't think that way'. Clearly this is another moot point...

I do know that managing your horse as well as you possibly can, so that his physical and mental health are optimal, and he therefore feels really good within himself, can certainly enable him to cope with herd life, help him to stand up for himself more effectively, if necessary, and be more inclined to do so. Feeling good or bad can alter a horse's view of life in general, and therefore his reactions to whatever he experiences in his interactions with others. If he has a meek and mild nature, then that is what he will always have; but good health generates self-confidence, and other horses do take notice of that.

9 Respond to your horse's changes of mood

Like all creatures, including humans, horses have moods and feelings, and they certainly do not always feel the same every day, or even at different times of day. Expecting our horses to behave like predictable, mechanical robots is foolish, of course, but it is surprising how many people react badly to a horse whose behaviour appears to be erratic, when he is only responding to something outside his control.

What causes a change in feelings?

Lots of things, and much the same things as in humans and other animals.

- The weather may affect the horse physically, and this in turn will put him in a good or bad mood. Some horses hate the heat whilst others hate wind and rain, particularly accompanied by cold temperatures.
- Hormonal changes are very powerful controllers of moods and feelings. Mares have a regular cycle, and when they are in season some of them can change considerably. Approximately 75 per cent of geldings retain stallion characteristics, which become more prevalent in spring and summer, the natural breeding season.
- In winter, most horses are naturally quieter if they are kept in natural conditions (saving energy due to lack of food), but horses kept for domestic use often become much more lively, usually because they are given too little work and turnout, and too much energy-giving feed. In summer, heat and grass have a quietening effect.

What can I do?

In general, the best advice is just to go along with it to a certain extent. Watch your horse's demeanour and behaviour, and handle and ride him or her accordingly. Particularly with mares, sensitive, quiet, firm handling is sensible and fair. Geldings who are 'silly' in the spring need a firmer, understanding hand.

If the weather is the culprit, you will need to manage the situation: thus if your horse feels the cold, exercise him in a warm quarter sheet and put on suitable rugs in the stable or field. In summer, try to exercise in the early morning, when it is cooler than in the evening, and avoid strenuous work in humid conditions because your horse will tire more quickly, and may even become overheated.

Many people say that horses must behave and work regardless of how they are feeling, otherwise they will just learn to take advantage of us. However, this is only true up to a point, and forcing an issue simply to make a point is tactless and foolish: you could end up on the ground; if the horse is not feeling 100 per cent you could become guilty of abuse, and if hormonal influences are the cause you won't override them anyway. Herbal calmers may be used, but not to replace correct management. Judgement, humanity and consideration are the answers.

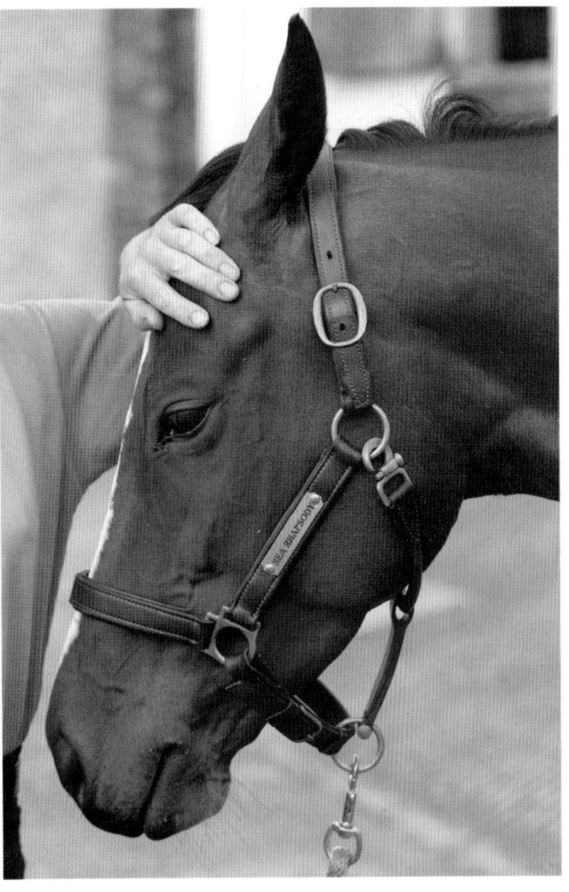

10 Graze your horse in hand

Horses live for grass, and are generally turned out with free access to it, yet some poor creatures never get any. They can certainly do well on conserved forages – hay, haylage, bagged and chopped grasses, straw and alfalfa/lucerne, plus some cereals if necessary – but grass is what they all want more than anything, with the exception of those horses brought up in regions where there just isn't any.

Why graze in hand when he has his paddock?

There are several good reasons. For a start, it means you are spending time together in a situation in which he is likely to be happy: this is always a good thing, because he is then more likely to associate you with pleasure – company and grass as well – which will certainly help to cement your burgeoning relationship. When his head is down he is relaxed, and this is an excellent state of being with which to associate you. You can add to this by occasionally stroking him low down on the neck and the withers, an action which is known to calm horses. (See also pages 8–9.)

Grazing in hand takes your horse into places that he may not otherwise experience, or may only pass through (eyeing the grass on the way!). The grass will taste different from that in his paddock, and possibly better if the latter works hard. There may also be different plants and herbs, all of which add to his mental satisfaction and provide a treat and valuable nutrients as well.

The more worldly experience he has, the more mentally and spiritually 'rounded' he will be. When he lifts his head for a brief – very brief – rest, he sees different views, may meet different people and animals, and become more used to traffic, farm procedures and vehicles and so on. Provided you pick your area and equip yourselves safely (see below), this is all to the good.

Although your horse will almost certainly be getting on with the main business of the hour, namely eating, this does not mean that he will take no notice of you. He may often give you a soft glance, or touch you with his muzzle as he raises his head with a mouth crammed full of delicious grass, and this makes you feel good.

A final excellent reason to graze your horse in hand is to compensate for the poor or non-existent grazing facilities provided by some livery yards, or at times when your own paddock is out of use.

All this gives the horse a chance to eat his birthright, provides a really enjoyable part of the day for you both, and is very well worth doing.

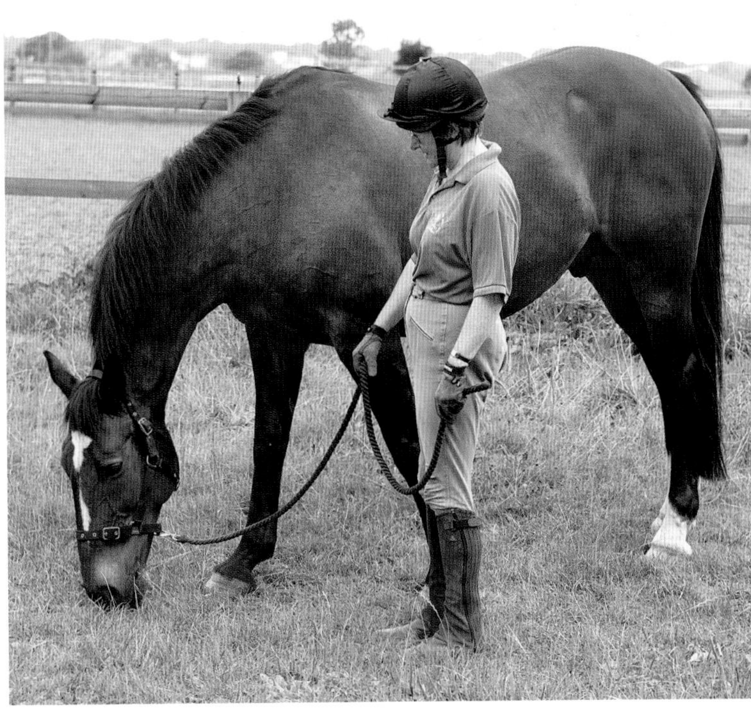

Take sensible precautions

Where you graze depends not only on the areas that are available, but also on how well educated your horse is in hand, and on how well he behaves. Taking him off the premises so that he can graze verges and other occasional patches of grass is all right in a quiet locality, but he needs to respond reliably to your commands and aids. It is absolutely imperative that he stands still, walks on and moves over at your request, both for your own convenience and for the safety of you both.

You both need to be as safe as possible, so you should wear your hard hat, gloves and strong boots, you should dress appropriately for the weather and have your mobile phone with you. If the weather is cold or drizzly, put suitable rugs on your horse, but make sure that the front fastenings are loose enough for him to get his head down in comfort.

Personally, I feel there is no point in grazing him in a bridle unless he is expert at manoeuvring the grass around the mouthpiece. Jointed bits are easier to cope with, but straight-bar or half-moon mouthpieces usually end up with a thick wad of grass wrapped around them, making the task of grazing impossible. Some insurance companies insist that horses led in a public place wear a bridle, so you may choose a jointed bit.

I am a keen supporter of nose chains (such as the Tellington chain lead), and find that you have more control with these, if need be, than you do with a bridle; but check with your insurance company. A nose chain (often called a 'stallion chain' because they are used for stallions, being so effective) means, of course, that the horse has nothing in his mouth that will obstruct his eating. A lungeing cavesson may be used, but horses cannot move their jaws freely in these if they are correctly fitted.

A long lead rope or a half-length lunge rein will give you more play should the horse become startled and leap about; it will give you more control in such a situation. A full-length lungeing rein can be cumbersome, but is better than a normal short lead rope.

How long should I give him?

Almost any time at all is better than nothing, but really as long as you can spare. When the horse first gets out he may eat apparently ravenously for a little while, but after that he will take things more easily. He will slow down sooner if he knows that he is going to be there for long enough to satisfy himself. However, if you are really rushed, 10 minutes is better than no time at all.

11 Introduce new things considerately

Part of a horse's survival mechanism is to be wary of anything new. Scientific research has shown that horses do not see as sharply as humans (and neither do our dogs and cats, surprisingly), and they identify shapes and movement rather than detail. This explains why they often baulk or shy at perfectly ordinary objects or the changed appearance of a familiar place. Sounds and smells also need investigation.

A matter of trust

One question that is asked frequently runs something like this: 'Why is my horse suspicious of anything new I introduce, or something different he sees out hacking? Surely he knows I wouldn't hurt him.'

Much depends on the existing state of your bond or relationship with him. It does take a great deal of trust and habitual co-operation with you for a horse to regard anything new or different with equanimity and show little or no reaction to it, because this is not natural behaviour for horses. Training can accomplish remarkable changes in behaviour, but you cannot change the horse's nature, which has evolved to avoid predation. Anything he regards as suspicious can trigger his 'flight or fight' mechanism, and we have to respect this.

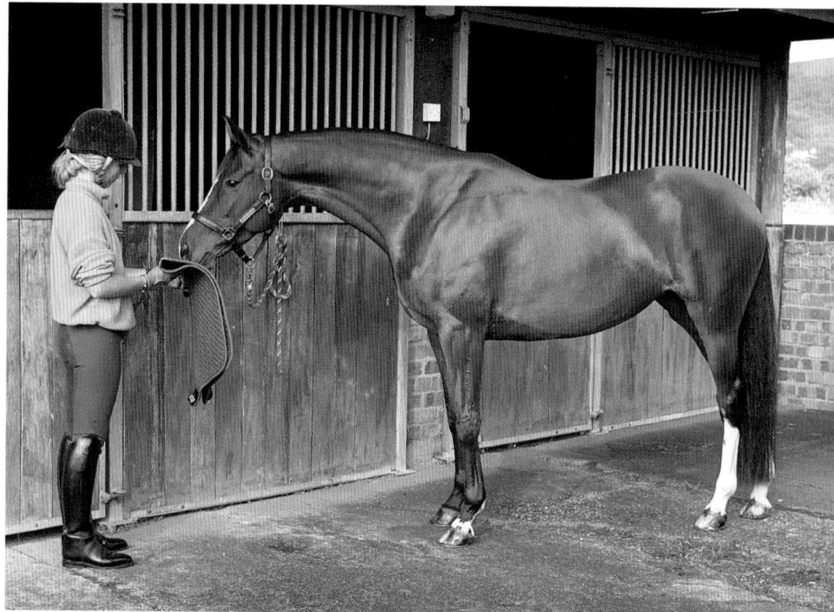

What can I do?

Remain very calm yourself and move slowly, quietly and confidently. New items can be made more acceptable by rubbing them with a piece of chestnut trimmed off his leg to make them smell of him. Alternatively, you can rub them with something which already smells of him, such as his numnah, rug or boots. An old tip was to rub things with a little of his own droppings or urine. When he has sniffed the item, let him see you rubbing it yourself and, very gradually, touch him with it on the shoulder. You can calm him with vocal reassurance but don't praise him until he is quiet.

When out and about in areas he knows and something unfamiliar has appeared, such as a new park bench, a line of new fencing or dumped rubbish, you will have to decide whether to let him stop and investigate – his natural inclination – or make him pass it by. If you stop, he'll want to approach (maybe snorting), then smell it, maybe feel it with a forefoot and perhaps walk round it; only then will he finally walk away satisfied. Your job here is to sit up and deep, and to stay relaxed. Keep a gentle contact with the rein, stroke him low on the neck and withers, and say whatever he associates with 'safe'; I use a long-drawn-out 'all right'. Do not praise him by saying 'good boy' whilst he is still worried about it, only when he accepts it.

Another viewpoint is to flex the horse away from anything suspicious, and keep him going (see pages 72–73). This may be necessary in, for instance, traffic or crowded places where you just cannot let him investigate the object freely.

12 Check his balance before handling

A classical tenet tells us to first position our horse so that he physically can do what we are going to ask, then ask him to do it, and finally let him perform the movement. It is pointless asking a horse to do something if he is not physically positioned so that he can actually carry it out. This also applies when working horses from the ground and in the course of basic handling. Many problems arise because horses are badly positioned and prepared, and are simply unable to oblige.

About balance and movement

To optimize balance and therefore movement the horse operates his four legs and feet in a different way for each gait. It is remarkable that a foal learns to manipulate his long, ungainly legs – almost as long as his dam's – and to run nearly as fast as her within 24 hours, but in the wild he would have to do this for his own safety. Thus the different patterns of his footfalls in each gait are programmed into him, as indeed they are in all four-legged animals.

Horses and ponies can also quite easily balance on three legs, as we all know; the other day I was picking out a mare's left fore foot whilst she was standing on her two right feet and resting her left hind foot on the toe, calmly munching haylage, supporting herself in effect on only her two off-side feet.

Establish the optimum stance

The most effective way for a horse to balance himself during any foot treatment is to stand with one pair of legs and feet, either the fore or the hind ones, level and straight down (not angled in any way), and the remaining third leg held straight down under the shoulder or hip. If a horse, and especially a young or inexperienced one, is not positioned in this stance, or at least somewhere close to it, before you ask him to lift up a foot you may well find that either he won't lift it up at all, or he won't hold it up for very long, because he doesn't feel himself in balance – and so it won't be his fault.

When asking a horse to move around, say in his box, look first at the position of his feet, and ask him to balance himself before you expect him to make a move, whether this is forwards, backwards or sideways. Not to do so – not to allow the horse time to balance himself – and to ask again, perhaps more assertively, before he is ready, can cause consternation in some horses, which does not make for calm trust.

If you want the horse to move his hindquarters to the right and he is standing with his left hind leg well behind his right one, for example, his instinct will be to either lean back and place more weight on his left hind leg then move the right one, or bring the left one forward and maybe under his belly, crossing over the right one. Even an everyday movement like this takes a couple of seconds, and horses not used to being stabled, such as a youngster recently brought out of a field, can have a problem with it at first.

This is just one instance showing the importance of patience and understanding in your relationship.

13 Be the person your horse turns to

Horses are notorious for needing other horses for company. They are herd animals, most of whom only feel safe with other horses or ponies around – or at least one other. Other animals such as donkeys, sheep, goats and even cats and birds may be tried as companions, and some horses have formed firm bonds with them – but how do you get your horse to regard you in the same way?

Is it really possible?

Although your horse will obviously never regard you as another horse, it is certainly possible to reach a stage where he regards you as an essential and protective, guiding influence in his life. Equine history abounds with stories of horses and owners or riders who seem to know what the other is thinking, who act as one, who behave like a well-suited couple, and so on. Furthermore, although this can take a long time, it can also occur quite quickly: you just hit it off with one another, 'click', or however you want to describe it.

Many owners who keep their horses at livery or on someone else's place, and who therefore do not see as much of their horse as the staff, feel that because they are only with their horse for a comparatively short time each day or week, they cannot possibly form such a strong connection with him – but this is not true. It can, and certainly does happen, because you will be giving off a different aura from other people.

Attitude

Your attitude to horses in general, and your own horse in particular, is crucial to forming a firm, close partnership with him. I feel that the attitude we need to cultivate is one of trying to ensure that our horses are as well cared for – and cared about – as we can possibly manage. Horses definitely pick up on human attitudes, and if you don't care deeply your horse will know it and a bond will never form.

There are a lot of 'users' in the horse world – people who only have horses so that they can, for instance, compete against other people, take part in a particular pursuit, or have something to show off with. However, the very best reason to have a horse is because you want one for his or her own sake, not because of what he can do for you.

People who are only users, no matter how talented they are as riders, will never become the person their horse turns to when he's in trouble or has a problem, because he knows they don't really care about him deep down, and he cannot rely on them for help or trust them not to hurt him.

Other owners who will never have a true bond with a horse, even if that is on their agenda, are those who:

- bully and abuse their horse in the name of 'obedience' or 'discipline';
- are power freaks;
- are weak in mind and character;
- are inconsistent in their handling and care of the horse, so he never knows where he stands and so feels insecure and confused;
- lose their temper with the horse;
- beat horses up and are generally harsh with them;
- treat horses as disposable commodities, there just to do a job;
- want a horse as a possession or status symbol;
- are not prepared to look after a horse properly, or even cater for his basic needs;
- are not prepared to ride well and sympathetically...

...and so on – you get the idea.

So then, your attitude needs to be one of deeply and sincerely caring about your horse, and of showing it by treating him appropriately and consistently – part of this involves firm, fair discipline. Learn all you can about horses, and be open-minded (not the same as being indecisive). Be your horse's guide, protector, educator, supporter, leader and friend. It's quite possible to be the first five and still be friends. Don't do anything to distress your horse without an excellent reason, such as uncomfortable veterinary treatment. Horses do understand when you're trying to help, and they do actually come to such people in times of trouble, not only with themselves but with their herdmates.

Time

Time is one commodity that working owners are very short of, but it is essential to spend as much of it as you reasonably can with your horse, not just doing his chores. My book, *The Horse Owner's Essential Survival Guide* (see page 151), gives plenty of ideas for saving time and money so you can actually be with your horse doing things you both enjoy and cementing your relationship.

If you are short of turnout, be willing to spend hours with him, grazing him out on the end of a lead rope, talking to him and enjoying each other's company. I always find this really relaxing and rewarding. Sit and read in his box or field. Lead him out for walks. Practise bodywork on him that he'll enjoy. Avoid as far as possible doing non-essentials he doesn't like, such as pulling his mane and tail, clipping him, making him uncomfortable with unsuitable or too many rugs, giving him bedding he doesn't like, food he doesn't like or field companions he doesn't like – or, conversely, separating him from his friends – and if you are in a livery yard that virtually forces you to do these things, move off it and find a kinder yard for him. He'll soon settle and make new friends in a horse-loving yard.

Everything boils down to these three things: Attitude, Caring and Time. ACT on those three things, and you'll both get there in the end.

14 Be your horse's main carer

We keep horses in all sorts of situations, and most of us have to keep them at livery because we do not have suitable premises of our own. This can be a good thing, because there is usually help available from staff or other owners when you need it; but equally it can detract from your relationship with your horse if someone else mainly sees to his comfort needs, whilst you mainly make him work.

Why is this important?

If you are trying to create a strong, all-round bond, relationship and partnership with your horse, which is what this book is all about, it makes sense to try to get him to associate you with all the aspects of his life in which humans, as opposed to other horses, are involved.

All horses must be handled at certain times by other people, such as the vet and farrier – and we must all know of instances when the horse behaves perfectly for them, but not for his owner (or vice versa)! Horses are obviously used to adapting to different people – very few of us nowadays breed our own horses and keep them for their lifetime – but to be really close to your horse it is best for him to see you as 'His Person', the main human in his life, whom he associates with pleasure, interest, fair treatment, safety, security and the provision of everything he needs.

In a natural herd structure, members do not keep coming and going, of course. No horse is only around in the evenings or at weekends, or goes missing for several days then suddenly comes back expecting to be welcomed without question. Yet we humans do this, and it is amazing that horses do adapt to it.

Provided you and your horse have a fairly good relationship between you, this sort of routine does no real harm. However, we are talking here about really strong bonds, and not just an acceptable but slightly superficial relationship that could be closer.

But I work all day, so how can I be his main carer?

If your horse is on do-it-yourself livery, you may be his main carer anyway. Even if a friend or the yard staff do him in the morning and at lunchtime if he's in, you probably visit him most evenings and do things with him that no one else does, such as riding, hacking out, schooling, grooming, a bit of bodywork and so on. This in itself is enough to single you out as 'different' and 'special' and probably makes you his main carer.

However, it is very easy to succumb to the temptation of saying to yourself more than occasionally, and especially in winter, that you really are too tired to go to the yard tonight, too busy, too whatever, and to ring someone else to bring your horse in or turn him out, skip him out, hay up, feed and water and all the other chores that have to be done and which take time and effort, not to mention the trip to and from the yard.

This is when the horse can start to attach himself to other people as much as, or more than, to you. It doesn't happen with all horses, and most are good at sensing those to whom they are special. It is a wonderful feeling when you arrive at your livery yard and your horse calls to you and to no one else: perhaps he has heard the sound of your car, recognizes your footsteps or, if the wind is blowing towards him, your particular smell. Perhaps you have said 'hello' to someone else on the way to his box or the field and he has heard your voice. Whatever it is, it makes you feel that you are special to him. This can often happen to livery owners who are their horses' main carers and who have built up a special bond or relationship with them.

Horses can also build up particular relationships with people who only see them, say, every few days, for example the Master's horse in a hunt stable, or a racehorse who sees a jockey mainly on race days. They associate them with specific, but only occasional, aspects of their lives: the more special bond for such horses is with their groom.

The 'one-man' horse

Occasionally you come across a horse who seems to be more of a 'one-man horse' than others, and it can only take a week or two for such a horse to transfer his allegiance to someone else, perhaps when you are sick or on holiday. They come to associate them, and not you, with having their needs met and, therefore, with their security.

One way to avoid this is to try to arrange for several different people to care for your horse during your absence, so that there is no one person for him to associate with more than others. If you cannot arrange this, another idea which often works is to send such a horse to another yard during your absence, maybe for schooling or a holiday at grass with other horses he knows. He can come home when you return, and because he associates you with his home yard he will slot back into his normal routine and you should have no trouble.

15 Establish a 'leader/ protector' attitude

We have already discussed the fact that some people, from a variety of backgrounds, believe that horses recognize 'leadership', and other people don't. This topic is mainly about the kind of attitude you have towards your horse. You are probably aware, without thinking about it, how you regard your horse and how he seems to regard you – and you may both be happy with this, or not.

Being in tune with your horse

We are all aware of doing things without thinking, reacting to and associating with other people and animals without thinking about our relationship. We 'just know' how we each regard the other. Sometimes we know instantly when meeting a new person or horse that we like them, dislike them or are indifferent to them. Sometimes our initial feeling about them is proven by experience, but sometimes we may change our mind – and all this can be done for the most part subconsciously.

Horses definitely know whether or not people are naturally in tune with animals. My first husband spent a good deal of time helping to train police dogs. He knew nothing about horses but could handle my Anglo-Arab gelding with no trouble. He just seemed to transfer the quiet, superior, no-nonsense attitude he had towards potentially aggressive dogs to a different large animal – my horse. Although the horse was easy to handle, he could be highly strung and would not respond to idiots; but he recognized my husband immediately as a 'leader' type, and they got on well together.

What can I do?

Although it is always a good plan to acquire as much knowledge about horses as you can, the above example illustrates clearly that you can achieve a lot simply by having the right attitude. Many horses feel insecure around people who are wary of them ('what's she afraid of, maybe I ought to be on my guard?'), so if you haven't already got the right attitude, cultivate it.

Practise giving out quiet strength and assuming to yourself that you are in charge. You know you are superior, and that's that! The horse won't argue! Expect the horse to do what you want. Tell him vocally, by means of your body position, and mentally that everything is fine, there is nothing to worry about because you are in control, and you are both going to do this (walk quietly to the field, get his feet picked out, trot down this track, walk into that trailer ...) and you'll almost certainly find that it happens. If you have a smidgeon of doubt, it may not.

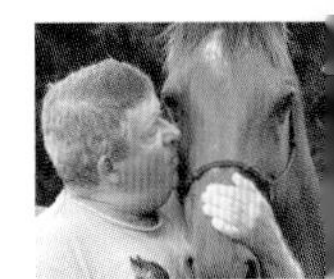

16 Be consistently trustworthy

We and our horses all have feelings: we are living, breathing beings, and we may feel like behaving in different ways on different days according to how we feel, our mood, what else we'd rather be doing, and so on. The problem with horses is that they can learn the tiniest or biggest things in one quick lesson. We only have to let them down once and they will remember it, along with all the times we didn't.

Consistent means...

... constant. A related word that does not appear to be much used these days is 'constancy', which itself means faithfulness or 'not changing'.

Horses understand and like constancy, faithfulness and 'not changing' because these qualities enable them to know where they are, where they stand and what to expect. They also enable horses to do something they are very good at: forming habits because they can rely on a situation. They give them some warning of what to expect and enable them to trust us, which brings us to...

... being trustworthy

Trustworthy means to have a firm belief in the good, personal qualities possessed by someone, to have a confident expectation that that someone will behave in a certain way to the good, or that a situation will always be the same.

From a horse's viewpoint, this means that the horse knows that a particular person makes him feel good and does not confuse, distress or hurt him; also that he will always find a comfortable bed, hay and water in his stable.

The practical implications

It is not easy to be consistent, particularly if you have a variable temperament. It can, or could, be quite easy on some days to lose patience with one of our horse's known quirks, to do up the girth a bit too quickly if we are in a hurry, to accidentally knock our horse with a bucket or allow a door or gate to close on him and hurt or frighten him.

If we want implicit trust from a horse we have to create it – unchangingly. If a horse knows for certain that he can rely on someone to always make him feel good and to never hurt or distress him, he reacts better to that person and does things better and more readily for them, than for someone who has already made life unpleasant or uncomfortable for him or who even gives the impression that they might, or that they don't know what they're doing.

To the horse, the first person is consistently trustworthy. He knows he can relax in their presence because he feels physically safe with them and mentally secure in their behaviour. When it comes to humans, they are where he wants to be.

17 Remember 'calm, firm and positive'

In the first book in this series (see page 151) it was stressed several times that the best approach to horses was to be calm, firm and positive. I can only reiterate it here because that attitude captures the essence of handling horses in a nutshell – what you need to be and, given a level of technical knowledge, how you will succeed.

Calm

Horses learn nothing when they are excited, apprehensive or frightened, because their prey animal's brain will then be completely occupied with ensuring their own safety and security. Even experienced horses may feel apprehension, because they know from past experience (with you or another owner) what is going to happen. Even if it doesn't, the excitement can remain as the horse waits for the anticipated event, and some horses may stay in a tense state all day, even when removed from the situation.

Many trainers and riders will insist on 'riding him through' his emotion with a view to 'teaching him that he has to behave', no matter what the circumstances. If the excitement or whatever emotion the horse is feeling is not too intense, this will work with some horses (although this is no time to try to teach new behaviour or movements, because he simply won't be concentrating); with others it will simply make them worse. There is no substitute for knowing your horse!

If you are competing and you feel that you really have to enter your class (and the horse is at least manageable), the best thing you can do is to stay resolutely calm yourself – which is much easier said than done. Horses usually take their cue from the people around them, especially their rider and immediate handler: keeping your seat and legs relaxed, your upper body and hands still, and your brain focused on the job ahead, is an enormous help if you can do it.

A scientifically proven way to help calm a horse down is to stroke or rub (not pat) him on the lower part of his neck and withers. This is known to lower the heart rate/pulse, which is always raised when the horse is excited, apprehensive or frightened. Getting him to lower his head also has the same effect, as does, obviously, letting him graze a little and keeping him away from whatever it is that is exciting him, if possible.

Firm

'Firm' does not necessarily mean strong, although sometimes stronger aids than normal may be needed to make an impression. 'Firm' definitely does not mean abusive or brutal.

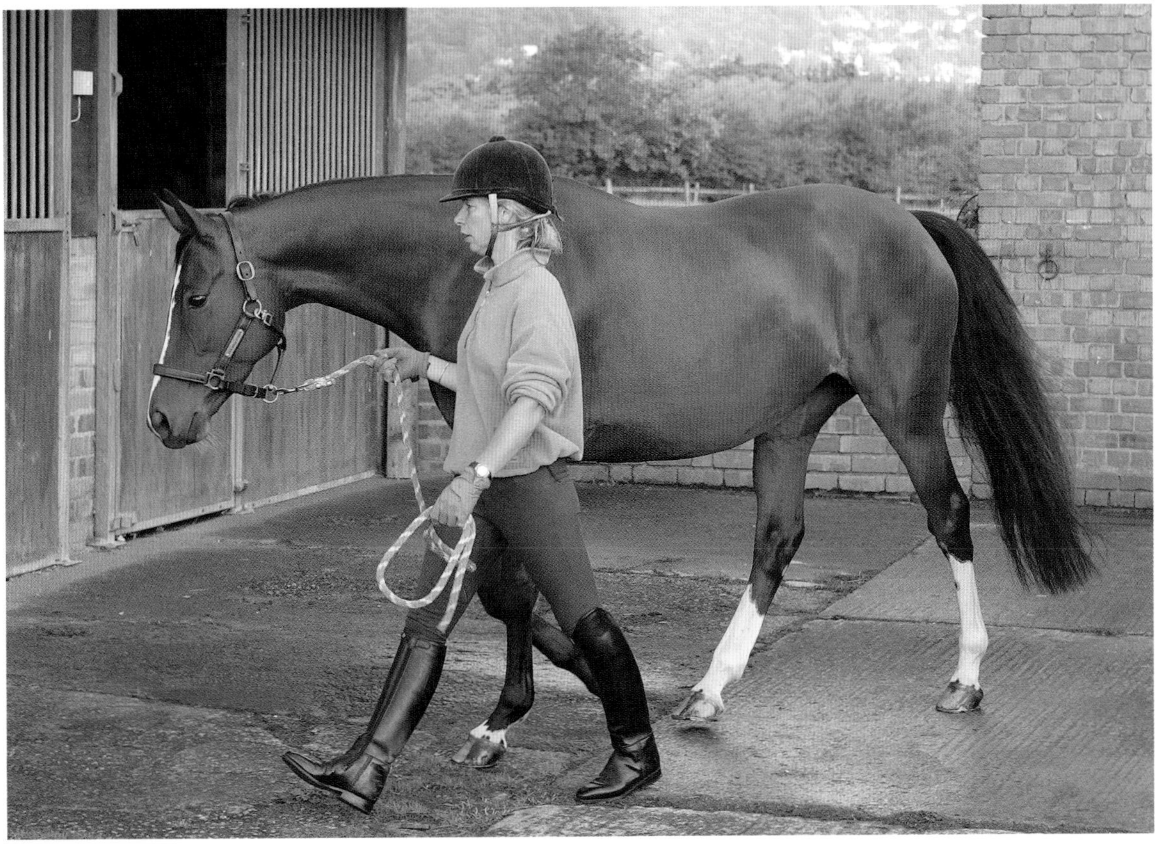

It can mean what I call 'persistent insistence': gently, patiently and unwaveringly continuing with something the horse knows well, such as passing through a particular gateway, across a familiar stream or going past a disliked pig farm to which the horse has suddenly taken stronger exception than usual.

'Firm' is also catching. Horses feel safer with calm, firm, positive people. They tend not to argue with 'firm', at least not for long, particularly when it is combined with quietness and calmness. If they have learned that you are always firm without being brutal, they are much more likely to co-operate because they have nothing to fear and they know you mean business. They take 'firm' as reassurance and follow its example: they tend not to do this with weakness, uncertainty, lack of confidence and negativity, unless they are a member of that increasingly rare group, the Traditional Schoolmaster.

Positive

The power of positive thinking has long been promoted as the way to succeed. It has to be tempered with realism, but with horses, if you believe or, even better, know that you will eventually succeed, your horse will tend to believe you and take comfort in your attitude. I am absolutely certain that we can picture to our horse what we want, and the horse will nearly always do it unless we stop him in some way, such as by sitting wrongly or inadvertently, using aids contrary to what our mind is telling him. Think and act positively in unison, and the horse will nearly always comply.

Horses find 'positive' practically irresistible. It is very hard to remain miserable or crotchety in the company of a pleasantly cheerful person, someone who talks good sense, is convinced that things will go all right, and who does not make a big deal of things. This is an ideal philosophy for working with horses.

In short...

... calm, firm and positive should be watchwords for anyone having to do with horses. There are others, of course, but these three generally encompass what you need to be. Like most things to do with horses, it does take a measure of mental self-discipline always to be like this, but most of us have experience of how horses react when we are excitable, weak and negative, and surely we don't want that again. Certainly our horses don't.

18 Foster mutual respect

'Respect' is a word I think both horses and humans understand, but they may have slightly differing views as to its meaning. If we respect someone it means that we probably pay attention to them, that we are considerate to them and also that we see their point of view, even if we don't agree with it. I imagine horses would possibly say that respect means a moderate degree of deference without being subservient.

A subtle difference

For an equestrian author, this is a tricky situation because this whole topic smacks of anthropomorphism (when human form or personality is attributed to gods or animals).

Anthropomorphism has long been, and usually still is, frowned on by most scientists and many animal trainers (although it is worth reading the two books by Dr Marthe Kiley-Worthington listed on page 151 for an alternative opinion). Obviously it is the personality aspect that causes these people particular problems – as far as horses are concerned, their inability to rationalize and their lack of logic.

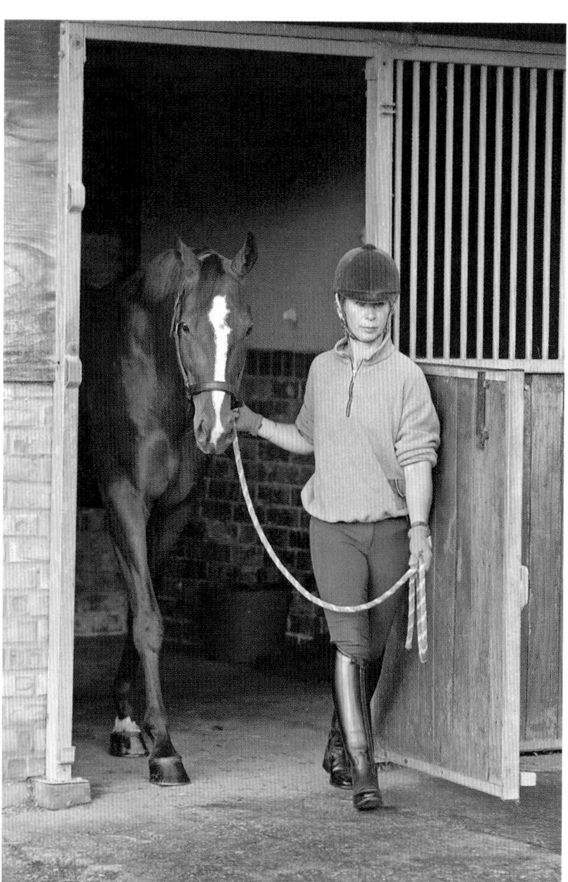

The particular region of their brain that controls these things is completely missing, it would appear.

Even if horses cannot show rationality and logic – and opinions vary on this, too – you don't need to be rational and logical to respect someone. We can pay attention to someone, be polite and see their viewpoint, without the qualities of logic and rationality. Horses regularly show a degree of deference to some humans and horses in their group, from foalhood onwards. They learn which creatures to 'respect' if their personal safety and position are to be maintained or enhanced because of how those others treat and react to them.

A logical, rational person will surely accept that, as mammals, horses are closely related to us, and are just as capable as we are, of physical and emotional feelings. Such people will also try to learn about the differences in physical and psychological function so that they know what kind of animal they are dealing with. Personalities differ in both humans and horses, so such a person will also make allowances for the individual horse in their care.

So how do I foster mutual respect?

Mutual respect can be fostered between a horse and a human by the human behaving and treating the horse in a manner the horse understands (so the human knows that the horse has really understood what he wants), and by the horse behaving in a polite manner towards the human so that the human's security and comfort are maintained and enhanced, and not compromised.

This does not mean that the horse cannot ask the human for something, or convey, in his own way – which we must learn to understand – his feelings; or that the human cannot give way a little and make allowances to the horse. Indeed, I believe this interchange is essential for a mutually respectful relationship.

19 Go for long-term ownership

Horses are living longer than they used to. A few decades ago, horses living and working into their late teens and twenties were in a minority. Not so now. Advances in veterinary care and nutrition have enabled us to maintain good health and strength for longer in our horses, and there is more interest in horses changing jobs, rather than being pensioned off as a former this-or-that or, indeed, being put down as no longer useful.

Buying, selling and moving home

It has always been quite common in the horse world to buy and sell horses as commodities. Many people feel that the horse is there to do a job, and if it doesn't do it, it goes. They, however, will probably not be reading this book.

People sell or re-home horses for many reasons, and sometimes this is unavoidable. They are expensive and difficult to keep decently, never mind well. But if you are interested in maintaining a strong, mutually beneficial relationship with your horse, it is well worthwhile making every effort to keep him, even when things become difficult in your life.

Horses and owners who like each other and get on well usually find that their relationship gets better and better as time goes on. One hears such expressions as 'telepathy', 'spiritual communication' and 'we just know what each other is thinking'. The less sensitive may ridicule these sentiments, but others will nod wisely and be glad that they will probably always have a stronger bond with their horse than their denigrators: they know something that the denigrators don't.

Ways of making it last

The main ways of making your co-relationship last are:

- Get to know as much about horse care and riding as you possibly can.
- Study and 'feel' your own horse so that you can understand him almost instinctively.
- Spend as much time, and lots of quiet time, together as you can.
- Take meticulous care of his health and happiness.
- If you fall on hard times, emotionally or financially, try to find help through a like-minded sharer, and work out ways of getting extra money and of spending less in general – a move to a cheaper yard may work out really well.
- Think ahead in terms of years. Never give in at the first sign of a problem. You'll be surprised at what you can both overcome if you try.
- Learn to manage problems you cannot cure. Life changes all of us, and not always for the worse.

Now that I've finished this list, I realize there are seven items in it, and seven is regarded as a number of magic and fortune. Magic is what a strong, long-lasting relationship is, and fortunate is what you both are, to have each other.

20 Don't aim for perfection – be happy with excellence

Not aiming for perfection relates to having a certain 'give and take' in a relationship and accepting the old, sound advice that no horse is perfect – and remembering that no human is, either. You have to accept your horse's limitations and your own, once you are certain what they are; this leaves you room to be human and the horse to be a horse.

Perfectionists

Why is perfection not something we should strive for in relation to horses? People are urged to strive for it in business, sport, artistic pursuits and life in general – but I think this is a great shame, because perfectionists miss some of life's most beautiful moments. Horse people might like to consider that even in one of the most popular of competitive equestrian sports, dressage, perfection is not expected. The top mark of 10 earns only the remark 'Excellent', not 'Perfect'.

Personally, I admire perfection when it arises, but I rarely relate it to human achievement, rather to a stunning sunset, an exhilarating canter along the edge of the sea, the sound of the dawn chorus. Perfection means 'faultless', and as we all know, there is no such thing as a perfect, faultless horse, pony or human. Anyway, perfection, like beauty, is in the eye of the beholder. By whose standards are we saying that something is perfect? It is interesting to remember that the two tenets by which the Knights Templar lived their lives were:

- Understand and live by the laws of nature.
- Learn to conduct your own life.

Setting your own standards is better than living by someone else's. Of course we need knowledge and guidance, and maybe coaching or teaching in order to know what is good or bad as far as achievement goes – but surely our level of achievement can at least be partly gauged against the circumstances prevailing in our own lives? Two riders each completing a show-jumping round, say, may be working in very different situations. For one, the round may be nothing particularly remarkable, but for the other the same level of performance may be the pinnacle of achievement.

Furthermore, perfectionists never seem to be very happy. They can be elated at a good performance and smile broadly, but each time this happens you can sense that for them, there is always something missing. Perfectionists:

- critise everything and everyone, and their own performance, even when it is excellent;
- pick fault with their horse even when he has done his best (which is all he can do);
- are difficult to work with, teach, learn from, or have as friends or family;
- are never satisfied with what they have done, and can't stop working at it;
- praise hardly anything or anyone;
- tend to think that their standards are higher than other people's (they are – they're impossible);
- tend to be selfish and stubborn.

No wonder they never achieve perfection!

The perfectionist's horse

The most important point in the foregoing analysis of perfection and the perfectionist is whether you can imagine the effect that the perfectionist has on his horse. Horses are animals who mostly just want a relaxed, trouble-free, interesting and comfortable life. Perfectionists achieve anything but that, and tend to transfer their frustrations and unreasonable demands on to their horses. Imagine being a horse and doing your best to understand and to carry out what your person seems to be asking, but being drilled, nagged and maybe coerced to do better and better, and to give more and more, constantly, and not knowing what you are doing wrong, until you know you cannot do, or give, any more. Your life at this moment has become almost unbearable (the anthropomorphism will help you appreciate that horses do know when they cannot bear any more).

Every time this person gets on your back you know, from past experience and by association with being ridden by this person, that you are going to be subjected to a significant period of physical and mental striving, stress and discomfort, if not pain – and you don't know when it will end. This is equivalent to what in past legal terms was designated 'mental cruelty' – and maybe physical as well.

Striving for excellence

People who 'only' strive for excellence are quite different. They are delighted when the horse does his best, even if he comes last. They, too, strive for the best performance of which they and their horse are capable, but are truly happy to come somewhere near it. When they mount their horse for a session of any kind, whether schooling, competing or hacking, the horse knows, again from past association, that he will be expected to work, but not to the point of pain, misery or exhaustion. He also knows that he will be praised and rewarded in a way he understands (see pages 68–69), and he will associate learning new things with interest and maybe a sense of achievement.

Give me excellence any day!

Riding, groundwork and training

Riding involves both of you

To be able to ride one's own horse is the dream of many people who ride at riding schools and centres, or who ride friends' horses. It is a dream being realized more and more as, in the UK at least, riding schools continue to close down and people who really want to ride buy a horse of their own or loan one.

This takes them into the realms of great responsibility, risk, expense and commitment, plus hard work, but also of tremendous satisfaction, fun, reward and, for want of a different expression, spiritual enhancement, provided they are the kind of owner who does not just regard the horse as a status symbol or merely a vehicle on which to prove their superiority to other people by beating them in competition.

Riding has been a popular as well as a necessary activity for thousands of years. If it is done properly (involving sensible riders on well-schooled horses) it is a fairly safe sport even at the faster gaits and over fences. 'Properly' means that the techniques used are effective, humane and safe, that the rider takes sensible precautions in what they wear, how they handle the horse, their choice of horse and what they attempt to do on that horse.

The horse, for his part, must be healthy, sound and comfortable, before being asked to carry a rider. This is a requirement for safety and for horse welfare. Horses who are in pain or uncomfortable do not work well, and may react by either 'closing down' (prompting stronger aids or even brutality from some people), or becoming resistant or even violent by bucking, napping, rearing and so on. This will destroy whatever good relationship you have built up because the horse will lose his trust in you, besides which it is inhumane, even cruel, to ride or work a horse who is sick, injured or in distress, discomfort or pain. (Poor riding and schooling techniques can also cause injury, distress, discomfort and pain.)

Six feet on the ground

Many people own horses but do not ride them. There are various reasons for this, but increasingly I find that it is because they have had problems and are now afraid of riding. In some circles there still seems to be a stigma attached to admitting that you have lost your nerve – but there is nothing wrong with having the sense to admit this. I have lost my nerve seriously three times in my life. The first two times it came back almost to normal, but the last time it didn't. I still ride regularly but am now much more careful about the horses I ride.

People who do not ride can still take part in various activities with their horses. Apart from driving, there are all sorts of groundwork techniques which are fun, which keep your horse mentally active and, if they are done safely and appropriately, keep him 'tuned in' to you. In this section we cover riding, groundwork and training in general, with a selection of topics for you to think about and try together.

21 Do plenty of dismounted work

Even if your main interest is riding, there is a vast amount you can do from the ground to strengthen your relationship or bond. One significant point in its favour is that the horse can see you, or rather all of you, whereas his view of you on his back, if his head is straight ahead, is limited to your legs and maybe your elbow area. He can certainly see whether or not you are carrying a whip.

In the stable

I believe that every horse should habitually step back and stand still when you enter, and not try to barge out or resolutely block your entry. He should move over when you ask, and generally watch where you are around him, and should not move about with no regard for whether or not he crowds you or bumps into you. These last actions are not signs of a good, respectful relationship.

For your part, speak before moving, and run your hand over him to where you are going. This warns him of your movements, especially if you are going behind him. Some say that you should always tie horses up before handling them and should never go behind them, but whilst I appreciate that this might be a good idea with 'unreliable' or strange horses, I'd hate to have to do it with a horse of my own because it is not a sign of mutual trust or respect.

In the field

When working on a close partnership, you obviously want a horse who is not merely easy to catch but who comes to call (see *100 Ways To Improve Your Horse's Schooling* on page 151), or simply when he sees you in the field. If a horse leaves his companions and comes to you, not expecting a titbit, he likes and wants to be with you. If he will also follow you around and do things you ask, or asks you to do things for him, such as scratch an awkward spot, these are even better signs of an already great relationship.

In the schooling area

This is the area your horse associates with 'work': let's hope he also associates it with interest and enjoyment. It is safe practice to ensure that you have good control by tacking him up with a lungeing cavesson, a nose chain or a bridle and, if necessary, comfortably fitted side-reins attached to a roller or to the girth straps of your saddle. (When used as a 'helping hand' for control, I fit them so that they only just create a contact with the bit or cavesson when the horse has his head in a natural position.) However close you are to each other, and however well schooled he is, horses are always unpredictable, and safety must come first for both your sakes.

Round and about

An extension to schooling in the yard and manège is to take him out into quiet surroundings, depending on your local area, not to graze, but to do a little in-hand manoeuvring to get him into the habit of always listening to you wherever you are. Tack up the horse appropriately, as described, and wear hat, gloves and strong shoes or boots yourself. Take a long schooling whip to indicate what you want, or to touch him lightly on the part of his body you want him to move.

If his equipment for these outings is different from what he wears when he is led out to graze, he will soon learn the difference (like a stallion always wearing a particular bit, only for when he is covering mares) and will not be constantly trying to eat grass instead of working with you.

Formal work in hand

Many classical trainers work their horses in hand before mounting, as this is a good way to supple them up initially before they have to carry weight. It is also sometimes easier to teach them movements from the ground first. You need your normal riding bridle and a schooling whip, and some people also put on the saddle.

Work the horse from both sides, starting on his best rein. If this is his left, stand on the left side of his neck between his head and shoulder. Hold the reins with your left hand near his crest in front of the withers, the left rein between your ring and little fingers, and the right rein between your index finger and thumb: you can then easily put pressure on one or both reins. Hold the schooling whip in your right hand: this creates forward movement with light taps where your left leg would go, on his thigh, rump or any leg you wish to move.

Start on the track on the left rein so that the fence controls his right side, tap, say 'walk on' and walk straight forwards, adjusting the reins so that his head is straight. You will soon get the feel of it and be doing lateral work, although lessons from a good teacher will always help.

Communicating with your horse in hand in the above ways gives an extra dimension of interest to your partnership and adds to the growing understanding between you. This can only help your relationship.

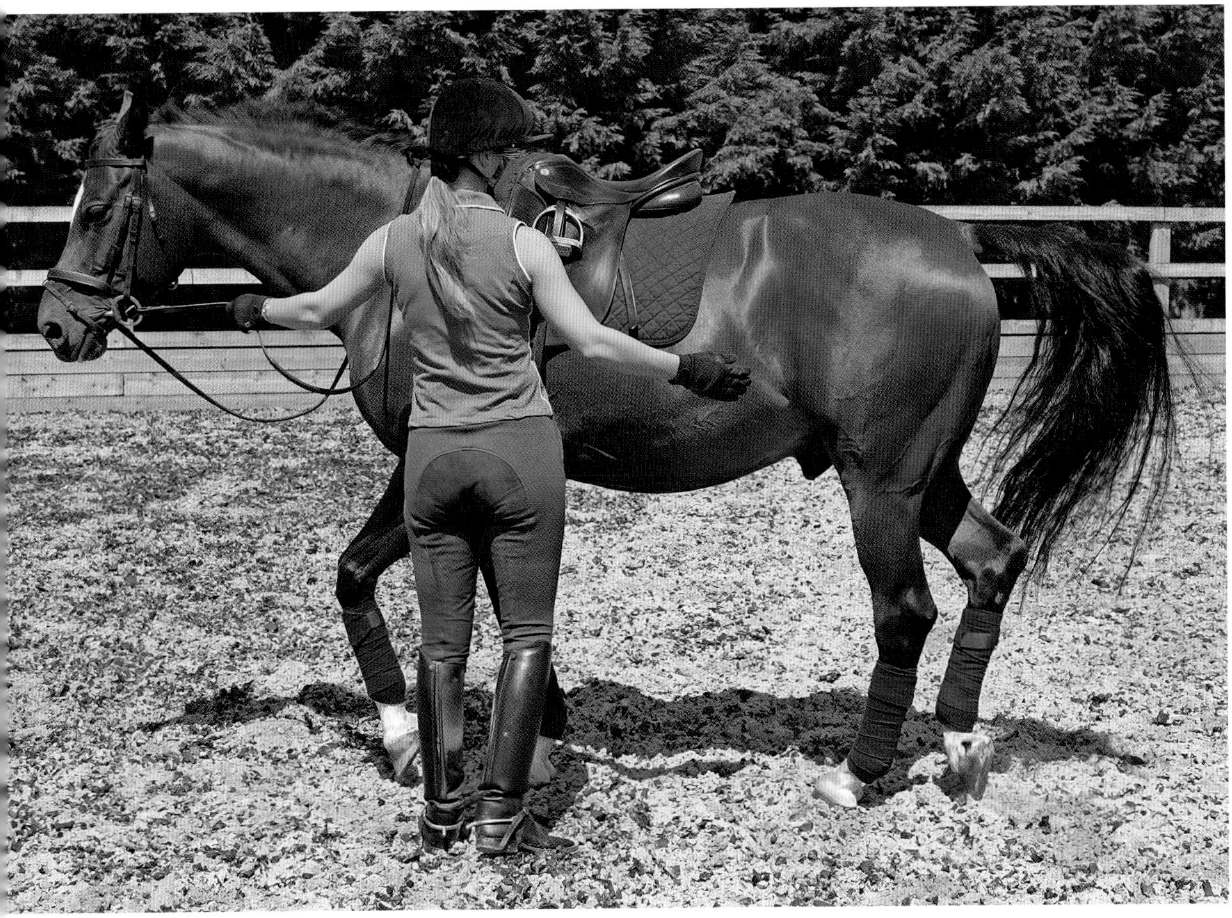

22 Try loose schooling

Many livery yards forbid loose schooling in outdoor manèges, and some even prohibit lungeing, in case a horse becomes too boisterous and damages the membrane. This is a great shame, because loose schooling can be a valuable and enjoyable activity for horse and owner, and any friends willing to help.

A school without a membrane

Membranes in schools can cause a lot of trouble, and a return to schools with a properly prepared base and no membrane would be a good idea (see *The Horse Owner's Survival Guide* on page 151). In countries that are drier than the UK, this is not a problem since working arenas are often of earth and sand.

Any surface, whether for dismounted or ridden work, needs to be slip-resistant and with a cushioning effect without being deep, the horse's hooves cutting in about an inch (2.5cm). It should feel as much as possible like the spring of old turf with its mat of roots underneath the grass. This is an advantage both physically and psychologically. Horses evolved on grasslands and their legs function best and are best protected on such going.

There is also yourself to consider. If you are working your horse loose, or doing any kind of groundwork, you will need to be able to walk and maybe run around the arena easily.

Deep surfaces are very hard to move on for both horse and human. They can cause stumbles if you cannot move your feet quickly enough, and slight soft-tissue strain in horses. They create a false, struggling way of going which is no good at all. Conversely, hard surfaces jar the horse's feet and legs and are painful to fall on!

All surfaces should be maintained in an even condition for safety and consistency of going. Most need regular harrowing and raking.

Preparing the scene

The arena needs to be prepared so that the horse cannot get out and cannot hurt himself on anything. If a horse is working loose and perhaps becomes rather excited, he may decide to jump out. The fencing, therefore, needs to be at the height of his withers or higher to discourage this. The fencing, and the gate to which he may gravitate, must be smooth on the arena side with no protruding posts, nails or bolts sticking out, splintered wood or anything else of that nature.

An excellent kind of arena fencing, rarely seen today because of the cost, is solid boarding or panelling that slopes outwards and upwards. This allows room for the rider's feet and legs when riding so they cannot possibly be caught or rubbed.

Round pens are popular and useful for horses you want to keep fairly close to you. But if you want to free-jump the horse they are too restrictive, and of course they offer no significant straight line for anything other than a single obstacle, nor do they give youngsters a break from working on curves.

Corners in some schools can be 'rounded off' by slotting jump poles across them, resting on the rails; this guides a horse round them and discourages him from finding an escape corner to go and stand in. Let's hope the horse won't actually want to do this.

Things to do

If you are loose jumping, the horse should wear protective tendon-cum-brushing boots or well-padded work bandages on all four legs, and overreach boots on the front that do not flop around and are not too long for his hooves. He can wear a well-fitting headcollar or bridle so you can catch him easily.

Obstacles are usually set up round the sides of the school, and there may or may not be a restraining rail or poles on the inside of the resulting lane. If there isn't, you may need a few friends placed around the school to stand quietly and still to guide the horse round the lane. The usual rules of jump construction apply: no protruding jump cups, tyres threaded on to poles or safely filled in if stacked, straw bales as fillers under poles only, not alone in case the horse banks them, and so on.

Any kind of flatwork can be done, of course. Some people use whips or ropes to instruct or control the horse, others just use their own bodies. Depending on the horse's temperament and your existing relationship, your body language can vary between being square on to him with an assertive posture, or less threatening, sideways on.

Your horse should be working co-operatively and willingly in hand before you loose school him. Do a little work on a lead rope first before taking it off, then just walk off, inviting him to follow you. Some horses are easily frightened by a new situation like this, and aggressive body language and shouting can terrify them. I personally do not believe in 'chasing' horses around unless they are genuinely lazy or uncooperative; the instant they do what you want, resume normal 'body language' and communication.

Once the horse learns to like this kind of work he should follow you around the arena and eventually work in response to your vocal commands and body gestures, jumping, working in patterns, standing and staying, coming to you and so on.

23 Teach your horse tricks

Tricks can be a fun way of building your relationship with your horse. To the horse, maybe everything we ask him to do is a trick! He doesn't know the difference between being asked for shoulder-in, jumping a fence and kicking a football. He just works out what we want, responds, hopefully with enjoyment, and accepts the reward. Ignore those who scoff at tricks – the difference is in the attitude of the onlooker.

The value of tricks

Tricks are something that absolutely every horse can learn. It doesn't matter what his conformation is, what defects he has, or what his 'real job' is or was. Although some may say that horses who do tricks are just responding out of habit to training, the horses do seem to know, perhaps from their owners' light-hearted attitude, that certain moves are different from, say, hacking out or working in the manège.

It always amazes me that many people have a low opinion of circus. They say things like 'that's just a circus trick' or 'that's no better than circus', showing their ignorance of the fact that circus was founded on superb riders and horses performing high school movements, as the best still do today – and better than many Grand Prix dressage combinations. People don't scoff at the Spanish Riding School, at police horses jumping through fire hoops and walking over 'bodies' or through lines of washing, or at the unbelievable moves performed by stunt horses, whether seen in films or at major horse shows. Yet there is absolutely no difference: these are just some of the many things we ask horses to do.

What can I teach my horse?

You can teach your horse almost anything provided you do it with a simple, step-by-step progression. The best trainers note what a horse has an inclination to do naturally, and build on it. Lots of horses like to imitate us. If a horse likes to use his forefeet, teach him to kick a football. Stand by him and push the ball with your own foot, saying 'kick'. Then lift his foot and push the ball with it, repeating 'kick' and immediately saying 'good boy' and giving him a titbit. He'll soon get the idea of what you want.

On page 151, three of the books listed – *Equine Education* and *Horse Watch* by Dr Marthe Kiley-Worthington, and *Classical Circus Equitation* by H. J. Lijsen and Sylvia Stanier – give plenty of ideas and explain the techniques.

Go ahead. You'll both have great fun and improve your mutual communication and understanding – and that can only enhance your partnership in the long run.

24 Keep your horse interested

We all know that we learn and enjoy subjects best if we find them interesting, but no matter how much we love something, there comes a time when we want a break. Although we humans have the mental capacity to keep on with something boring or stressful because we know that it's good for us, horses and other animals do not. If we want a real equine partnership we have to create interest and enjoyment.

The horse's attention span

Some years ago I was taking a course on learning to teach, and was interested to learn that the attention span of humans for the continual absorption of information was 25 minutes. Humans are supposed to be among the brightest animals on the planet (yes, debatable), so where does that leave horses? Many scientists claim that horses do not operate so much by intelligence as by habit and instinct, so perhaps we may conclude that their attention span is much less than that of humans. Sensible, sensitive trainers have long advised that we keep sessions short, for good reason.

We know that horses learn quickly if they have a reason. They are motivated by a reward such as escape from their box or field or a food treat/praise (see pages 68–69) from the trainer, or by simply learning to do something enjoyable such as jumping free or galloping in balance under a rider. Once the horse has learned something, there is no need to keep teaching him as he will probably do it in a mentally detached way, as we might do when typing or driving a car.

Drilled to death

Consider, then, the mental state of horses who are drilled round and round a manège for many minutes at a time – 30 to 60 is quite common. They must be only half listening to their riders, performing the same boring things over and over again. By association, horses must come to dread these ordeals, and they must feel even worse when harsh, confusing riding methods are used.

What can I do?

Consider these points:

- Do not drill your horse in movements he knows already.
- To keep life interesting, try to teach him something new during each short session.
- Horses retain information best if you train a new movement only once a week, it seems, not even twice, as this gives time for new neural (nerve) pathways to form in the brain.
- You can establish work already learnt out on a hack or in some other environment.

25 Don't expect more than your horse can give

Horses have traditionally been regarded as big, strong animals, and the phrase 'as strong as a horse' has pervaded our everyday conversation for generations. However, they are also flesh and blood, and can be sensitive and highly strung, not to mention nervous and easily frightened sometimes. They become concerned over daunting tasks and demands just as we do, and can also lose their nerve.

Are you sure he can do it?

Today, many people are looking for a quick fix for everything. If they see something they want they want it now, not tomorrow or next month. If they have a goal, they likewise rush and push to reach it quickly – but the problem is that such people rush and push their horses, too, and this is a sure way to destroy trust and destroy a relationship that has taken months or even years to build up.

Sometimes, asking more of a horse than he can give or is ready for is done unintentionally. It is not always easy to assess when a horse is ready to move on in his training, and the help of a sensitive teacher can be invaluable here. It is important to ask why the horse is having a problem, even though you are fairly sure he knows what you want. Could this be because:

- he is not fit, agile, strong or supple enough – and if so, why not?
- he is getting older and is just starting to be unable to work as well as he used to?
- he is being taken along too fast in his training, and it's all too much for him?
- vital elements were missed out of his training earlier so certain important work has never been established, and what you are asking now is a stage too far?
- whatever you are asking is associated with something frightening in his past and he just cannot face it now?
- he has reached his limit of individual talent or propensity, and never will be able to do what you are asking, no matter how persistent you are?

A fragile trust

All these things, and others you may think of, are excellent reasons for reluctance or inability. If your plans and goals exceed your horse's actual or potential capabilities, you are in for disappointment at some point unless you modify your aims. Most horses need only one unpleasant, frightening or uncomfortable, painful incident to change their view of their owner. This may become immediately obvious or may build up over time, especially if the demand keeps on being made by a person who does not sense that they are pushing the horse too far. Trust is a fragile thing. Treat it gently.

26 Enjoy fun activities together

Surprisingly, to me at least, not everyone rides for fun. Horses are no longer needed for war or ridden transport in Western countries, so no one has to ride them. Therefore, if someone doesn't enjoy riding, surely they could find something else to do? Horses definitely pick up on our moods, and if you are not having fun your horse will know, and he won't be happy, either. This atmosphere can erode the best partnerships.

I have my horse for a particular discipline

Having your horse for a particular discipline is fair enough, but this book is about forging a close partnership with your horse, a mutually beneficial relationship, a firm 'bond', to use current terminology. No matter what discipline you wish to take part in, if your horse doesn't enjoy it, none of those things will happen because he will associate you with having to do something he dislikes, through all the degrees of that.

You may still win prizes together, but that is possible between a horse and rider who don't even know each other very well. It even happens between horses and owners who don't get on brilliantly. That is not what we're aiming for when we are trying to develop a close and trusting partnership between horse and human.

What can I do?

It's best to find out what your horse enjoys doing and does well, then build on that. If you want to compete or take part in organized activities, there are disciplines to cater for all tastes and inclinations, so it should not be difficult to find something. If your horse enjoys an activity, he will probably have fun.

One activity you can take part in together, and which most horses take pleasure from if you pick your area and maybe travel to it, is to hack out on a ride, sometimes just the two of you, and sometimes with friends, provided your horse gets on with the other horses. Many horses and riders do not hack out, but this does not mean that you couldn't, with a bit of training and organization. You can go on picnic rides or planned short or long tours of an area, finding out which inns and hotels cater for refreshments for horses and riders. Organized trail rides take this a step further.

You can do fun things at home such as groundwork, little (or large) obstacle courses and relaxed lessons in a different style of riding.

Having fun together means mutual enjoyment, which always creates happiness, interest and pleasure in each other's company.

27 Use your voice a lot – correctly

Anyone who has spent any time observing and studying horses cannot miss the fact that they are quiet animals. They communicate mainly by smell and body language – they are extremely perceptive of even the tiniest movements and vaguest attitudes. We are primates, and studying other primates, including humans, highlights a main difference between our species and other ones: we can be deafening to them!

Well, I talk to my horse all the time...

Talking to your horse is good if you do it thoughtfully. Horses pick up on, and learn, not only words but tones of voice. To the horse, of course, whatever we say is all just a sound. You need to get him to associate a particular sound with a particular action or emotion.

Chatter can be as annoying to horses as to many people. Chatterers are thinking of themselves, not about the person or animal who has to put up with it. As far as horses are concerned, they clearly have not thought about how their chatter sounds to the horse, and have completely overlooked the fact that the horse doesn't speak English or any other spoken human language.

Although chattering is not the best way for someone to communicate with horses, they can pick out certain very familiar sounds from amongst the jumble, sounds which really mean something to them – like 'carrots'! However, chattering puts them under the irritating slight stress of having to really concentrate in order to pick out anything meaningful. This is not the best way to communicate with a horse or get him to relax in your company.

... but my friend hardly ever talks to hers

It is a sad fact that not many people talk to their horses. I find that this stems from not being allowed to speak to a horse during a dressage test (other than the tests of the Classical Riding Club), which, in turn, probably comes from the early days of eventing. It was devised as a test of a military charger, which may have needed to work at night quietly and was taught to obey physical aids only.

The voice conveys a tremendous amount to horses, who have superb hearing for all nuances of sound. The tone of your voice can frighten a horse, calm him, energize him, relax him, give him confidence or make him wary. Correctly used, the tone and the word/sound combined are a truly invaluable aid in your dealings with your horse.

What can I do?

It's a good plan to restrict yourself mainly to an initial vocabulary of words or very short phrases such as his name and 'stand', 'back', 'foot up', 'over', 'walk on', 'trot on', 'canter', 'easy', 'no' and 'good boy' or 'good girl'. 'Head down' is also invaluable on the ground or from the saddle. These cater for most eventualities. The way to teach them is basically, you ask for the action with physical aids, then the instant you get it, say the word so that the horse comes to associate the sound with the action. Then quickly praise the horse (see pages 68–69). Once it is learned, the word alone will produce the action – provided your horse has an amenable nature. Even if not, it still works, provided that complying has become a well-established habit with your horse. (See *100 Ways to Improve Your Horse's Schooling* on page 151.)

Dr Marthe Kiley-Worthington has been working for over 20 years with a mainly home-bred herd, now in its seventh generation, in an effort to learn more about educating equines as opposed to simply training them, and also what it might be like to actually be a horse. As far as learning human words and phrases is concerned, she and her team have found that horses can learn very many more words than the 'starter list' given above, and also variations of words and phrases such as 'go right', 'go left', 'go out', 'come here' and even 'lift your right leg' and 'lift your left leg', and many more. She also notes that very few people praise their horses when they have done the right thing, but they nearly all tell them off for doing the wrong thing – a very telling and sad way to behave, though I am quite sure that readers of a book such as this will not be guilty of possessing such an attitude!

A lifesaver

One of the most interesting and beneficial things you can do with a horse is to work him loose and get him to respond to just vocal commands and suggestions. You have to be really disciplined yourself to stand absolutely still, not even lifting a finger or using your eyes for direction, if you want to be sure it is your voice that your horse is responding to. Stand relaxed and still, and use your voice in a consistently familiar way as regards sound, inflection and tone. Your horse must be already well established in responding to your voice in other circumstances. This 'ultimate response' could potentially save lives in dangerous situations, such as your horse being loose on a road or in a showground. In such a situation his name, plus 'stand' or 'whoa', are best. A still horse is a safe one.

28 Don't play mind games with your horse

Of course, all your horse's experiences with you involve his mind. By 'mind games' I mean unfair ones that confuse, anger, irritate, panic or frighten your horse. Most people would not do this intentionally but, due to not knowing precisely how to act in specific circumstances, a lot of harm can be done to the horse's mentality and, therefore, to his trust in you and to your relationship.

What do you mean exactly?

See what you think of these rather extreme but real examples. They both illustrate a complete lack of understanding (or caring) of how horses' minds and bodies function.

A woman arrived home from a show, roughly shoved her horse into his stable and, complaining that he had been useless, got into her car to go home. Her friend asked about feeding him and the owner replied: 'No, he can go hungry tonight to teach him a lesson.' Obviously the horse could not possibly connect the two, so the friend fed him and left him comfortable, making him feel better and probably averting a case of colic due to digestive disruption.

A girl was whipping the legs of her horse, who was tied up, every time he moved. He was very agitated, and I asked her why she was doing it. She said it was because another owner had told her to do it as a punishment every time he moved. But they had both entirely missed the larger picture, which was that in punishing him in this way they were effectively connecting, in the horse's mind, being tied up with fear and pain, so making the problem worse and creating others. I tactfully explained what she could do instead, and at least she stopped whipping him.

'A little knowledge is a dangerous thing'

There are various methods of expertly promoted horsemanship that are currently very popular, but problems arise when people follow them without understanding equine psychology and behaviour first, and so are unable to gauge the merits and logic, or lack of it, of each system. It is also important to be able to assess your own horse, because not all methods suit all horses.

Many people like to take parts of systems, and also use some of their own ideas and some from conventional training, and devise their own way. This is fine for very knowledgeable, sensitive and 'thinking' horsemen and women, but it can create major problems for others and their horses.

What can I do?

Again, it is back to learning as much as you possibly can yourself. Re-read page 12, observe with an open heart and mind as many horses as you can, especially your own, and read the books on page 151. Study the horses produced by anyone you plan to learn from, and eventually you will know what road to follow.

29 Hack out, if at all possible

Many riders would love to hack out but daren't because they feel that their surrounding area is too dangerous because of the traffic, and/or their horses are not good in traffic. There are also just a few horses who actually do not like hacking out, maybe due to a frightening experience in the past or because they sense nervousness in their rider. Both can be improved with patience and retraining, however.

A change is as good as a rest

The old cure (which still applies today) for stale racehorses and others was to give them a season's hunting. The comparative lack of pressure and stress, the slightly lower level of fitness needed, and the excitement and fun of being out and about and doing different things with a 'herd' of other horses would bring about an apparently miraculous change in a horse's outlook and performance, creating a renewed zest for life and for his 'proper' job.

Hacking is less structured and organized than hunting, of course, and most horses love it, particularly when done in company. It is an enjoyable way of giving the horse a change and a sense of going somewhere. It can lead to your taking part in organized pleasure and trail rides, competitively or not, and so of being able to ride in country you would not otherwise see, which all adds to the enjoyment.

How can hacking benefit our partnership?

Out on a hack you can come across interesting and sometimes testing situations which strengthen not only your riding skills but also, believe it or not, your confidence and your horse's, too. When you have learned a few techniques about hacking (see below), you will really feel that you have achieved something together, and this seems automatically to bring you closer together with increased respect, trust and empathy.

What can I do?

If you already hack – get out more! If not, try seriously to retrain yourselves to cope with the situation in your district, if at all possible. A book called *The 100% Horse* by Michael Peace (*see 'Further Reading'* on page 151) will help you. You could also research areas in your immediate vicinity to which you could transport your horse and enjoy good hacking.

With horses not used to riding out, you probably need to find others to go out with. If you don't know anyone, make a few enquiries, put an advert in your local horse magazine, or put up cards in tack shops and feed merchants' premises, stressing that you are looking for a well-behaved companion or two to set your horse an example. This way you can also make new horsey friends.

30 Be consistent, logical and rational

We have talked about being consistent with a horse several times already in this book. Consistency is important whether or not you believe that horses learn by association and habit only, or are capable of thinking things out – or both. The horse needs to know where he stands for a calm, relaxed life. But what about logic or rationality? If horses don't operate this way, do we need to do so?

A bit of logic – maybe

There is no difference between logic and rationality. Logic is the science of reasoning or rational thought, of thinking things through in a chain of connected thoughts that come to a (reasoned) conclusion. This ability, so definitive of reasonable, sane human beings and a few higher primates, is one that horses are claimed by many not to possess – but not by everyone.

We do need to behave logically, because logic and reason enable us to think things through and avoid making mistakes with our horses, and to treat them appropriately for their species. As a friend of mine pointed out, if we, as creatures of supposed higher mentality, do not behave this way, what hope could there be for anyone else? I could only agree.

Scientists often state that until something is proven to be so, we cannot assume that it is (which, being 'reason'able, does not mean that it isn't). Following this logic, until something is proven *not* to be so – for example, the common statement that horses are not able to reason – we must assume that it is.

Horses do not possess the parts of the brain that control reason in humans. This, apparently, is why we can safely assume that they do not have this ability. But as there is a very great deal we still do not know about the brain, we cannot be certain that this function is not controlled by some other part of horses', and other creatures', brains.

Example 1

Years ago, having read in all the standard horsey books that horses have no reasoning power, I tried my Anglo-Arab gelding with a little test of logic. I filled his normal feed bucket with feed and put the lid on, which I had never done before. I put the bucket in the yard and let Royal out of his box. He approached the bucket, smelled it to confirm the presence of feed and, after a very few seconds feeling the lid with his lips, took the round handle on top of the lid between his teeth, lifted the lid off, dropped it on the floor and ate the feed. To me, this shows that the horse had to:

- check by smell the presence of feed;
- realize that he could not get at the feed because of the lid;
- realize that he had to find a way of removing it, so he
- investigated the lid and identified the handle;
- thought of actually picking it up by the handle with his teeth (rather than just bashing the bucket about 'hoping' the feed would be exposed) and putting it to one side, so that
- he could eat the feed.

To this creature of supposed higher mentality (your author), this is a chain of connected thought which came to a reasoned conclusion – otherwise known as logic.

Example 2

My friend's son liked to perform what he called a 'scientific' test with her horses which he called the 'Carrot Test'. He would have a large carrot in one hand and a small carrot in the other. The carrots would be held in different hands, sometimes the same distance from the horse; but sometimes the smaller carrot would be held nearer the horse (so as to make it look bigger, Tom reasoned) and the larger one further away (so as to make it look smaller). No matter where the carrots were held, the mare always went for the large carrot and the two geldings always went for the nearest carrot.

Does this test indicate that the mare reasoned that she would get more carrot if she went for the bigger one, and that the geldings reasoned that they would have to make less effort, and get some carrot more quickly, if they went for the nearest one? It seems like it to me. It could also indicate that mares are more intelligent and geldings are lazier.

What has this to do with my partnership with my horse?

The foregoing analysis simply means that, yes, we should be logical and rational in our dealings with our horses because it has not been conclusively proven by assessing their behaviour that they cannot reason. If even one horse in the world can reason, we cannot say that horses have no reasoning power, so, thinking this through logically and rationally, it follows that they might be able to.

Furthermore, it seems that on many occasions they *can* use reason, so if *we* don't, they might come to the logical and reasonable conclusion that we are stupid, or at least have no reasoning power and are not (following it through in a chain of connected thought) rational creatures of higher mentality. (So *that's* the reason why so many horses treat their owners as inferior beings!)

31 Make mounting comfortable

The way some riders get on their horse must constitute one of his most uncomfortable experiences, and he goes through it every time they get on. He is led to the mounting area, and even if the rider uses a block, they often pull the saddle over, pull on the reins, poke the horse in the ribs, kick his hip or croup as they swing over, and flop or even bang down into the saddle. It shouldn't be like this.

A better way

Mounting should be done with care and regard for safety and the horse's comfort. No horse will welcome being ridden if he associates it with insensitive handling and discomfort.

Mount from a mounting block or something similar whenever you can, no matter how fit and agile you are – unless you can vault on, that is. There are times when we all need to mount from the ground, but generally this is not the cleverest nor the best way. If you do, get someone to pull down on the far-side stirrup to keep the saddle level: this prevents uneven pressure on your horse's back and strain on the saddle, not to mention being better for your own back and your horse's mind.

Try this...

Lead your horse to the block, with the girth only just tight enough to get on and with the stirrups down; gather your reins in your left hand if mounting from the left, with a gentle but definite contact on the mouth and the horse's head flexed slightly to the right so that, should he move, it will be towards the block, not away from it, leaving you in mid-air.

Putting your right hand on the pommel or waist/twist of the saddle – not the cantle, as that can twist its tree – try to put your right leg over it without using the left stirrup, and sit down gently. If this is not possible, rest your left hand, holding the reins, on the withers with your whip (if carried) down the right shoulder. Use your right hand to steady the stirrup and, once your foot is in place, hold the pommel as you spring up from your right leg, swinging it over well clear of the horse, and landing lightly in the saddle. Find the right stirrup with your foot, check that your leathers are flat against your shins, and remember that the girth may need to come up another hole.

A final thought

Whichever side you normally mount from, accustom yourself to mounting from the other side as well. This is good training for you both, in addition to evening up any stress on one side of the saddle.

32 Breathe in rhythm with your horse

If you swim, sing or practise yoga or Pilates, you will be good at controlling your breathing. If not, breathing in rhythm with your horse may feel a little strange or even difficult at first, but this has definite holistic, and many say spiritual, advantages. You can always do it surreptitiously if you think people might laugh at you! No matter what others may think, breathing really can bring horse and owner closer together.

About breathing – yours and his

Air is crucial to life because it enables the horse to 'burn up' the fuel in his blood provided by the digestion of food. Lack of oxygen can cause brain damage and death very quickly, but a free supply of clean air helps the whole body to function optimally.

Many people are surprised to learn that there isn't much difference between the human's respiratory rate and the horse's: our resting rate is about 12 to 15 breaths per minute (in and out counting as one) and the horse's about 8 to 16 per minute, so synchronizing your breathing isn't really all that difficult.

The horse can breathe at whatever rate he needs at walk and trot, but at canter and gallop his breathing is tied to the rhythm of the gait so that he breathes out every time his leading leg lands, and in during the moment of suspension.

How do I start?

The best way to start is by standing quietly in the horse's stable, behind him and a little to one side so you can watch his opposite flank rise and fall; or hold the flat of your hand against a nostril and feel his warm breath as he breathes out; or hold a mirror to see how often it mists up.

Once you have the feel of his rhythm, stand by his head (try to face him away from the door to avoid distractions), and breathe in time with him. Don't touch him or, of course, speak, and you'll notice that before long he will probably look at you, or feel as though he is more 'with' you. Relaxing sessions like this of a minute or so at a time do bring you together.

When riding, it can be difficult to synchronize at walk and trot except on cold days when you can see the mist, but you can always do it at canter and gallop. You'll also get a feel of how difficult it can be for him to be forced to breathe in accordance with his gait's rhythm.

33 Depend on your seat, not your hands

As primates, we use our hands a lot; also our eyes, looking at what we are dealing with. Unfortunately, these techniques are not the best way to ride horses. We get much better results if we develop and rely on our seat for balance, direction and security, and look ahead to where we want to go, rather than down at our horse – a real 'sea change' for many riders.

The importance of an independent seat

The term 'independent seat' was familiar to all students of riding even up to a generation ago. It describes a rider with a seat that does not rely on the reins either for balance, directing the horse or their own security. Strangely, many people believe that the reins are there to be used to help them balance and even to stay in the saddle, and this false belief is widespread. Hanging on to the reins will not keep you on in an emergency, but a firm seat in good equilibrium in the saddle will, in all but exceptional circumstances, as will the ability to keep your balance in accordance with your horse's movements, which is part of an independent seat.

Jockeys all ride with much shorter stirrups than other riders, and their horses are fighting fit and often explosive; yet the number of falls they take is minimal in relation to their circumstances. The reason is that a good race jockey, whether on the flat or over jumps, has brilliant balance. He needs to have because he can't rely on his legs and seat to keep him on: his stirrups are too short and his seat rarely touches the saddle. Just think how much more secure you will be in your kind of riding with the advantage of your legs and seat as well as terrific balance.

Your seat comprises all your underbody area *plus* the insides of your thighs – everything that is in contact with your saddle. Your lower legs can be wrapped around your horse (if long enough), but if you tense them up and tense the muscles of your thighs and seat, you'll find that this actually lifts you up *out* of the saddle, weakening your seat. Because your muscles are hard and stiff you impact against your horse's body, rather than your seat being absorbed into his movement, and are likely to be jarred up and off the saddle altogether.

Where do my hands come in?

Of course you need your reins on a jinking, cavorting horse, but rather to control his speed and head position and, therefore, extreme movement. You do this by means of *intermittent* pressure on the reins, not unrelenting, which many horses rebel against. They may slow down but often start going upwards, sideways, backwards and even downwards instead. Hanging on to the mouth via the reins encourages the horse to pull back hard and also gives him something to lean on.

How do I acquire an independent seat?

If you can get a good teacher or an experienced, sensible friend to lunge you on a reliable, calm lunge horse who will maintain a steady gait on a predictable circle, this is ideal. There are two body techniques to grasp – stretching up from the waist, and dropping down from the waist.

- Practise stretching up your trunk above the waist, shoulders back and down and chest raised a little and holding it there, firmly but gently, in an upright position. Your elbows should be at your hips, not in front of them, as this can incline your body forwards. Look ahead with your eyes, well round your circle.
- Practise, ideally without stirrups and in walk at first, completely loosening your seat, thigh and leg muscles. Raising the toe and pushing the heel down, stiffen the leg – loosening the seat and legs, including your ankles and feet, allows them to drop so that your weight is concentrated on to your seat bones. Gently push your seat bones forwards slightly and allow your loose lower body to absorb the movements of your horse.
- To take this on to sitting trot, read pages 88–89.
- In canter, whether on a bend/circle or straight line, the horse's back on the side of the leading leg is slightly in advance of the other side, so by placing your seat bone on that side a little in front of the other one you are sitting in accordance with the way the horse positions his back. This makes life much easier for him and, ultimately once you get the feel of it, for you. Don't rock with the canter: concentrate on sitting upright, even thinking a little backwards with the shoulders and balancing on your seat bones. Stay relaxed but firm and keep your legs dangling, letting your horse rock underneath you. If you stay open-minded you'll soon get the hang of it.

Also read pages 60–61 for further information. With practice and mental application, take this on to riding off the lunge and with stirrups, and your safe, secure and independent seat will surely develop.

34 Make sure his tack is comfortable

Tacking up is something most of us do almost without thinking, whereas it is something we ought to do with the utmost diligence. It is part of our horse's care, an element we are concerned about, not just something we do as a means to an end. It is a process that can be uncomfortable and directly affects a horse's well-being and welfare, both of which are top priority to an owner wishing to establish trust.

Consider his feelings

Whatever you plan to do in the saddle, the way a horse feels in his tack sets the tone for the whole of the activity. If he is uncomfortable, in pain even, not only is he going to associate it with being ridden, but also he will not be able to concentrate on his job and won't be able to do his best. As for your partnership, your horse is going to associate working with you with displeasure.

We assume that an experienced riding horse will accept wearing tack, but a little imagination will bring home just how uncomfortable tack can be if it does not fit or is inconsiderately adjusted. Let's look, then, at some good and bad points of tack fit – something that concerned horsemen and women who are keen to establish a strong rapport with their horse will regard as of great importance.

Saddles

The type of saddle you buy depends on what you want to do. Whatever the design, it needs to fit so that it does not hinder your horse, for that is the most you can hope for. The saddle needs to help you, but it will never help your horse: fitting a saddle and riding a horse is always a damage-limitation exercise because horses always go better with no rider or tack – you only have to watch and work them at liberty to be assured of that.

Many saddles these days, even some very expensive ones, are made with flat underseat panels. No horse has a flat back unless he has strange conformation, so such saddles are unacceptable because they 'bridge' on the back, concentrating pressure in front and behind but bearing little weight in the middle. You need a saddle which follows the slightly dipping shape of your horse's back, exerting pressure as evenly as possible from just *behind* the shoulders/withers to just in front of the loins, and from side to side, with no contact with the withers or spine.

Most synthetic saddles cannot be altered because they have preformed stuffing in the panels. Saddles with other forms of stuffing can be altered by a competent saddler, *but the inherent shape of the saddle still needs to follow the smooth, slightly dipping shape of your horse's back.*

It must also be the right width for his back and have a generous bearing surface. We have gone beyond the fashion for narrow trees and bearing surfaces that concentrated pressure on a small area of the back. These became popular in the mistaken belief that they made it easier for the rider to sit around the horse because the thighs could remain closer to him. Narrow trees have caused immeasurable agony to many horses, also muscle atrophy (wastage) due to excessive pressure squashing

blood vessels and thus inhibiting blood supply, especially just behind and below the withers where most of the pressure occurs in saddles that are not well made, adequately padded or accurately fitted and/or are too narrow. The tree points and stirrup bars are in this area, so weight and pressure are concentrated here. A saddle that is too narrow perches up on the back and is tight when you try to slide the flat of your fingers underneath the panels at the front.

Of course, a saddle that is too wide will rock from side to side and can cause bruising at the sides of the withers and spine; it may also press down on them, causing pain. You can fit padded numnahs under them to take up some space, but you cannot do this with excessively narrow saddles, as this simply makes them tighter, like thick socks under tight boots. So this is only a stop-gap solution until a qualified saddle fitter and a qualified saddler have put things right.

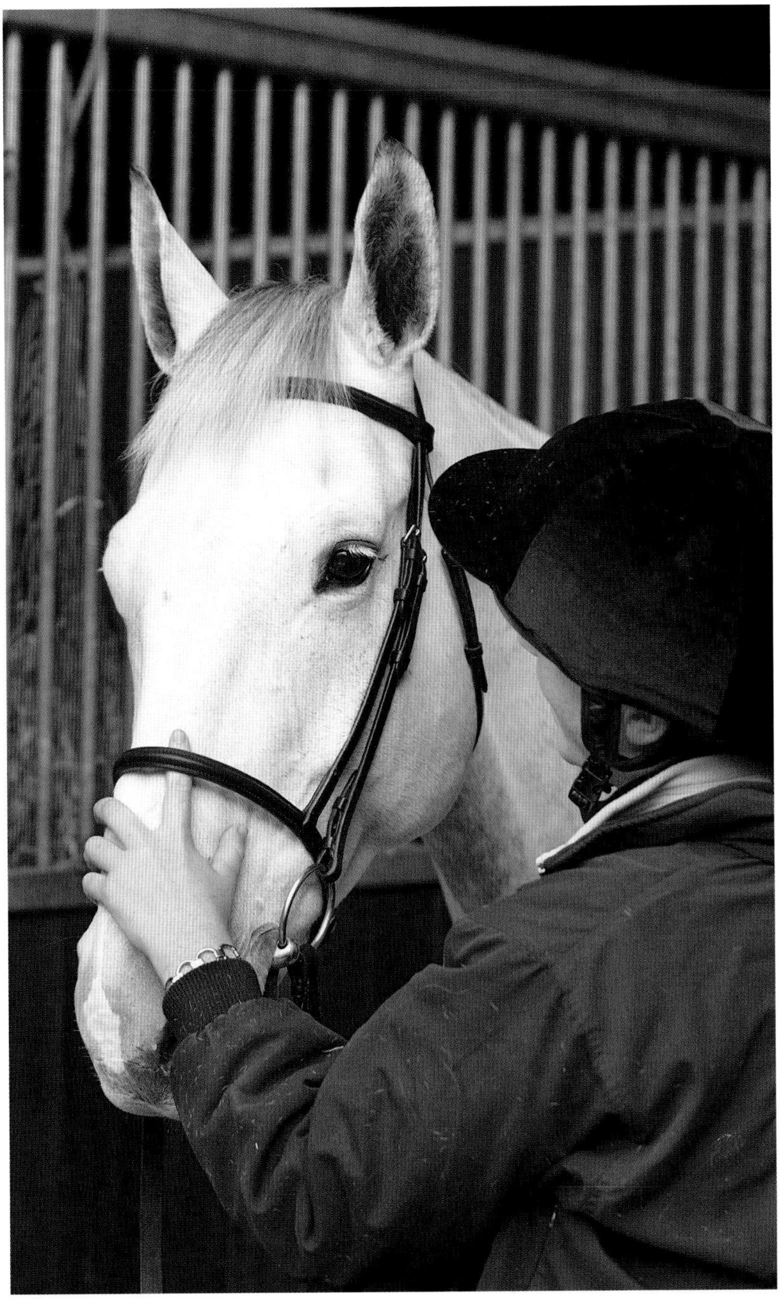

Girths

Whatever girth you choose, it must leave a hand's width of space behind the elbow to encourage and allow free, forward movement. I prefer those with a central elastic insert or an insert at both ends, either of which allows for even expansion when the horse breathes in so that the saddle is not constantly pulled to one side.

Bridles and nosebands

- You must be able to slide a finger easily all around under every part of the bridle including the noseband (the front being the telling point) for a comfortable fit.
- You must be able to fit the width of your hand between the throatlatch and your horse's jawbone, with your hand at 90 degrees to the jawbone.
- Jointed snaffles must make one wrinkle only at the corners of the lips;
- half-moon mouthpieces must touch the corners without wrinkling them; and
- the curb bit of a double bridle must not touch the corners at all, and lie about half an inch (1cm) below the bridoon (snaffle).
- A curb chain or strap must lie down in the curb groove and allow the bit cheeks to come back to form a 45-degree angle with the line of the horse's lips, when the chain comes into action.

35 Girth up slowly and carefully

A girth is like a tight strap around your chest (your ribcage) just below your armpits. No matter what it is made of or how it is fitted, it will inevitably, to some extent, restrict the expansion of the horse's ribcage and lungs, and will therefore obviously restrict his breathing. No one has yet designed a girth which both keeps the saddle in place and permits full, unrestricted breathing – a sobering thought.

The effects of conformation

A desirable conformation point in a horse is a natural girth groove a little way behind the elbows. You'll see a slight rise here into which the girth fits conveniently, helping it and the saddle to stay in place. If the horse also has

- 'well-laid-back' shoulders (where the spine of the shoulder blade forms a 40- to 45-degree angle with the ground), with the point of the elbow underneath or just in front of the highest point of the withers;
- moderately high, well-defined withers that are very slightly higher than, or level with the croup, so as to discourage the saddle from slipping forwards; and
- a well-sprung (moderately rounded) ribcage behind the saddle flaps, to discourage the saddle from sliding back on him...

then you have a horse who can 'carry a saddle'. He should also have no problems with the girth digging in behind his elbows at every stride as the forelegs move back. Even without this conformation, a good saddler and fitter can keep most horses' saddles in place without your needing to use a point strap in front of the girth straps, which can cause significant restriction and discomfort.

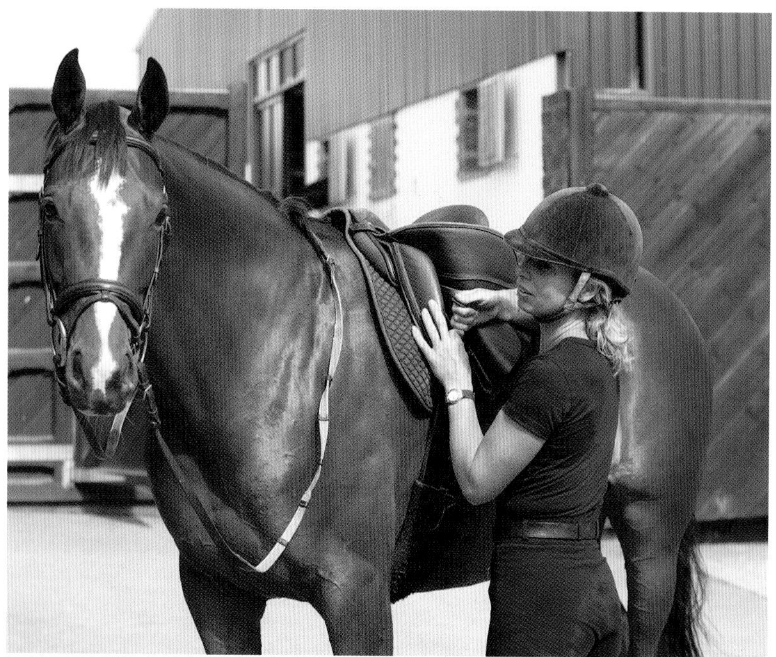

Placing saddle and girth

The shoulder blade rotates around a point about a third of the way down it; the top goes back and the lower part moves forwards when the foreleg extends. Place the saddle so that the front is behind the tops of the shoulder blades (immediately behind the withers) by the width of the side of your hand *when the foreleg is extended fully forwards.*

Place the girth down the saddle flap and go round the other side. Bring the girth up, fastening it to the girth straps so that you can easily slide your hand under it. Whilst the horse is getting used to this, put some other tack on him.

Fasten the girth a hole at a time between putting on other items, such as boots, from alternate sides so as to create an even feel. Ultimately, the girth should be just tight enough to keep the saddle in place whilst you mount (from a block, to be considerate to the horse).

Pull the forelegs carefully forwards and *down*, supporting knees and fetlocks, to smooth the skin, and check the girth when you have warmed up for about 10 minutes.

36 Realize that horses *can* be retrained

Horses retire from their disciplines or jobs all the time. Time was when a horse who was no longer able to do the job for which he was bought was 'retired' – and often left in miserable conditions – or shot. Now people are much more inclined to put a horse into different work, although problems can arise when those involved in the horse's new life treat him with preconceived ideas related to his old job.

Easing up

In our society, most horses are required to be more or less athletic. People breed and buy horses for specific disciplines with possibly little thought about what they will do when they can no longer fulfil their required task. Usually horses pass down the grade of athletic demand, from very athletic pursuits to less demanding ones, but sometimes it is just a sideways move.

The point to keep clearly in your mind when dealing with such a horse is that (with a few exceptions) horses can nearly always be retrained to be useful doing some job other than their original one.

Many people are concerned that, having become well used to one particular rider or style of riding, a horse may not adapt to a new person or system. This is hardly ever the case. The horse's previous job may have taught him useful things such as travelling (any performance horse), hacking out (particularly racehorses, eventers and hunters because of the need for roadwork), jumping (if you want to jump in a different discipline) and so on.

Even if the horse is well established in a way of going that you dislike or do not want, such as being heavy in the hand, going too fast, not listening to seat aids, pulling like a train and so on, it is still possible to reschool him to establish new habits (and therefore be more comfortable under saddle).

The work done by racehorse rehabilitation charities is a clear example of highly strung, often nervous, super-fit athletes learning that what is wanted is a more relaxed way of going and different techniques: these must be consistently and sensitively taught.

Horses with bad manners on the ground – which are often defensive habits learned for self-protection – or habitual behaviour that has become ingrained because no one has taught them any different, can often and quite quickly, in a matter of days or a very few weeks, learn different behaviour patterns with consistent training and treatment from their new owners.

Horses with significant problems, such as rearing, serious shying, determined bucking and bolting or 'charging off', can more often than not learn new ways with a combination of veterinary checks and treatment, firm and fair management, and positive, non-brutal riding techniques. Horses are very adaptable and natural lifelong learners. Take advantage of this fact.

37 Try to ride classically: it really works

We hear a lot about classical riding these days, as if it had only just been discovered or come back into fashion. Most people misunderstand it, and many are not really sure what it is or how it differs from 'ordinary' riding. Unfortunately, some denigrate it as being a technique apart from, and irrelevant to, riding today. In fact, the truth is quite the opposite, because its principles are relevant to every equestrian discipline and every rider at every level.

A definition

I find that it is helpful to define classical riding more as an ethos than as a specific system of techniques. Here is my personal definition of modern classical riding:

- Classical riding is a logical, humane system of riding resulting in mutual lightness, harmony, co-ordination and balance in horse and rider, which is spiritually uplifting for horse, rider and onlooker.

This, I hope, clearly indicates that there is no 'rough riding' or handling, no distressing mental or physical techniques, no forceful coercion and nothing that will confuse, upset or frighten horses, browbeat them, take away their spirit or make them feel insecure. Nothing is done that forces horses to move in ways that cause mental distress or physical discomfort or pain. If anything like this is detected, the rider or trainer is not following true classical principles, no matter who he or she is. In any relationship with a horse there has to be mutual safety and discipline but without bullying, cruelty or browbeating.

(For a fuller description of the methods, techniques and attitudes of classical riding, *see* page 151 for details of other books in this series and those by other authors.)

Why is the word 'classical' used?

The reason classical riding is called 'classical' is because it stems from what is known as the classical period of history, the time of the ancient Greeks and Romans. The ancient Greek cavalry commander, Xenophon, wrote *The Art of Horsemanship*, which is still in print today.

Down the ages, various riding masters have added to and refined the system, sometimes digressing from it in that their ways are too harsh, but it is still mainly based on a way of riding that gave riders in war security of seat, manoeuvrability, and a living weapon in the form of their horse who was trained to, on command, protect his rider and deliver blows and kicks to the enemy, as in the famous airs (movements) above the ground. For all these things, rider and horse needed qualities still found in good classical riding today: mental control, superb balance and physical suppleness, plus, for the horse, correctly developed strength. You cannot achieve these without a strong partnership between you.

Another important role of classical riding was, and is, to train horses to herd cattle safely, specifically the aggressive black cattle of the Iberian peninsula. In war, the rider rode mainly with the left hand (the bridle hand), leaving the right free for a spear or other weapon. In stock work and war, the riders often needed both hands free for bows and arrows or ropes, and the horses were trained to work from seat and leg alone.

Classical riding today

Of course, people often think that classical riding only relates to the more advanced or 'fancy' movements such as the airs or movements above the ground, as well as pirouettes, passage, piaffe and so on. This is not so, however: it is the techniques that are classical and the way in which the movements are achieved. You can often see advanced movements performed in non-classical ways. (It must also be explained that although many riders and trainers say that they teach and ride classically they do not do so in practice, although I accept that some of them believe they do.)

Learning the classical way

Any rider who wants to be more than mediocre would do very well to learn to ride classically. This does require mental and physical discipline of both horse and rider, as does anything worthwhile, but the results and the sense of achievement from the beginning onwards are exhilarating.

Classical riding is not some esoteric form of riding that few people, horses or ponies can master or need. I have ridden in several different ways, and I always return to classical. Little children can be started classically (I was four years old), and *any* riding horse will perform better with the qualities instilled by classical training.

There are, confusingly, several schools of classical riding both in thought and practice, not only at formal national academies, such as the Spanish Riding School in Vienna, Saumur in France and the Portuguese and Spanish academies, but also set up by individuals who may have trained at one or more of these establishments or been taught by someone else who did: many such people start their own classical riding centres or teach freelance.

To learn more about classical riding and training, read the books listed on page 151, and look in horse magazines for advertisements for classical centres and riding schools. Join the Classical Riding Club, based in Scotland but of international extent, detailed on page 152.

38 Warm up correctly

No sensible athlete would begin physical work without loosening and warming up his body. Today, the science of sports psychology involves his mind as well. In the horse world, those owners and riders of performance horses, whether competitive or not, who are also concerned horsemen and women, take the trouble not just to warm up, but also to learn the right way to do it.

Is there a wrong way, then?

There is definitely a wrong way, and we see it often. So many people, both at home and away at an event, bring their horses out of their stables or vehicles, tack up at once and take them into the manège or warm-up area, bringing them into an 'outline' almost immediately and going quickly into trot. They seem to expect the horse to 'go correctly' almost from the start, which is unreasonable and foolish.

So what is the right way?

Before you tack up, do a little hand-rubbing and stretching. Hand-rubbing involves using the flat of your hands, working with the lie of the hair; it stimulates the skin and the muscles immediately underneath, encouraging blood flow and helping to prepare the horse mentally for work. Gentle stretches, forwards and backwards, of all four legs, and of the head and neck up, down and to both sides, start the loosening-up process. A few minutes walking in hand with the horse's head down completes this stage.

In the saddle, spend a good five minutes walking out (without nagging for speed) on as loose a rein as you dare, depending on whether the horse is likely to shy. Ideally, have a completely free rein held at the buckle so that the horse senses no restriction if he wants to drop his head right down and stretch it out from time to time as far as he feels comfortable, stretching and limbering up at the same time. Guide him with the weight and pressure of your seat and legs, just vibrating one rein occasionally or turning by tapping his withers with your outside hand if necessary, and putting a little weight into your inside stirrup, and changing rein frequently. Do the same thing in a steady trot, trying to keep him in balance with your body posture and thighs, then try canter.

You may need to adopt this warm-up regime gradually. Horses that are not used to being given their heads adapt fairly quickly and become more 'thinking', much better balanced and thus more agile. Allowing the muscles to be relaxed ('decontracted' as a French-speaking trainer of mine would say) enables blood to flow freely through them, preparing them for the next phase – working in – when you ask the horse to come into hand and to start working a little more gymnastically before the serious work begins.

39 Cool down correctly

Cooling down is just as important as warming up. It was always considered a sin to bring your horse home hot, and it is, indeed, bad management practice because during work waste products, such as used-up body cells, carbon dioxide and maybe lactic acid, are formed and need to be cleared from the muscles. In addition, nutrients, fluid and oxygen need replenishing so that the horse can rest and relax comfortably and recover.

Under saddle

If your horse has become very hot and has been blowing, let him half get his breath back, then ride or lead him around at a slow trot for just a minute or two to keep the circulation going, removing those toxins and servicing the muscles with nutrients and oxygen. Then come down to a brisk walk on a loose rein.

Careful stretches after work help to ease out tiny knots of muscle that have cramped up around little injuries. Nature's response to protect a stressed or injured area is to 'close ranks' around it to prevent further movement, but this can actually increase the area of sore, hardened tissue, so doing stretches does help.

Ride the horse in walk on a loose rein with his head down for about five minutes, and encourage him to walk small half-circles, bending round your inside leg to left and right. The forelegs need to cross in order for the muscles on the outside rein to stretch. Guide him with your seat and legs, as in warming up.

In hand

Loosen the noseband and girth, and walk the horse out in hand, wearing a sheet or rug, or not, depending on the weather. The object is to cool him down but not chill him. Sloshing lukewarm water on him will help, and will refresh him in all but cold weather.

When he feels comfortably warm to cool, *and his breathing is back to normal,* you can put him away with some hay or haylage, feeding him later.

'Breaking out'

If your horse breaks out in a sweat after you have settled him down for the night, you will have to rub him down, change his rug and possibly walk him round gently for a little while. Breaking out can be a nervous reaction to exciting or worrying work, or it can be due to excessive tiredness or exhaustion, or lack of fitness. Make sure he has an electrolyte supplement to support his metabolism, and a small ration of easily digested food, plus enough fibre and water.

Watering

During the cooling-down process, he can be offered a few mouthfuls of water every few minutes, maybe with electrolytes in it if he will drink them; however, do not leave ad lib water with him until he is cool and breathing normally.

40 Use the aids correctly

Aids are not commands: they are signals that tell your horse what you want him to do, and help him to understand, the word 'aid' meaning 'help'; they are not irresistible stimuli that guarantee to produce a desired movement. For him to understand aids, a horse must be taught what they mean. They must not frighten or confuse him, and they must be placed and timed with precision according to his stage of training.

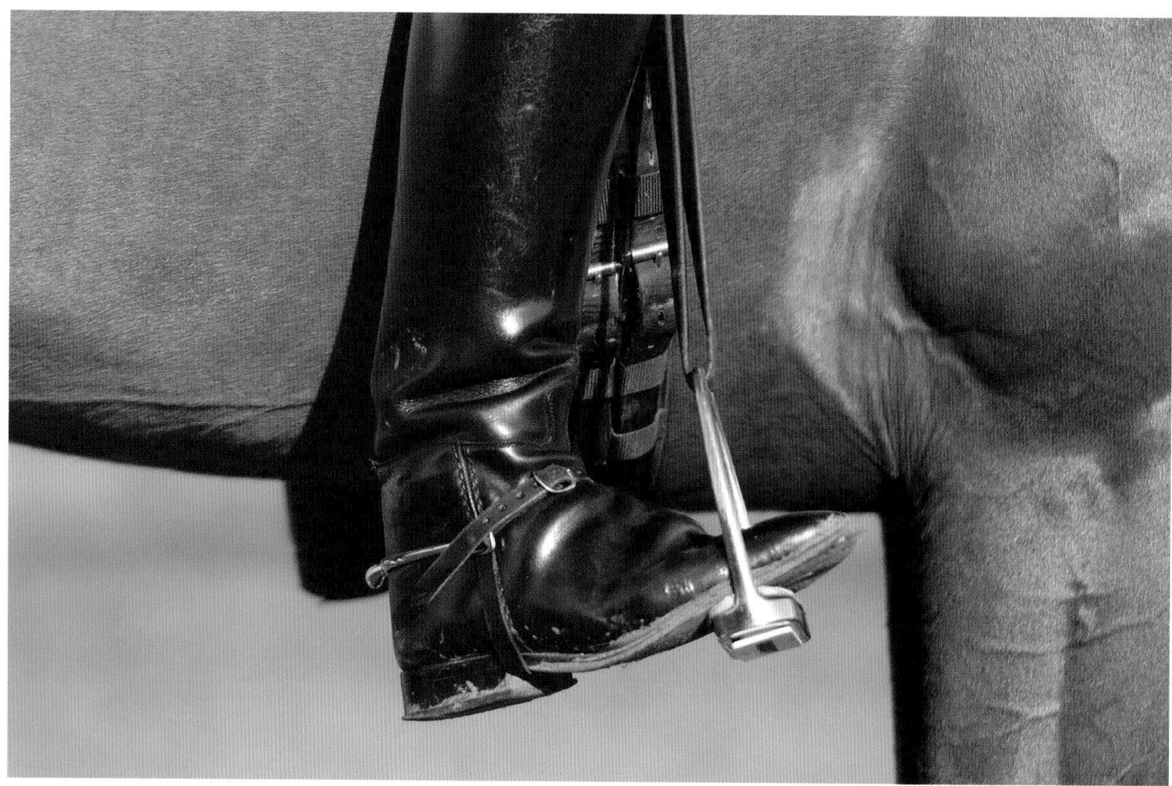

The nature of aids

The type of aid you use on a horse will vary according to his progressing level of training. If a horse is trained knowledgeably and sensitively, he should respond to lighter and lighter aids as he becomes more advanced.

If the horse understands what you want but is not responding, there is something to be said for giving an aid with as much strength as is needed to get a result, particularly in situations where the horse simply must obey for safety reasons, such as in traffic or where there are crowds of people; however, aids given harshly descend to the level of abuse or cruelty. Most horses, if logically and sufficiently accustomed to responding to aids, will eventually answer light aids out of habit. If the horse is frightened or excited, however, stronger aids may be needed, and even these may be ignored because of the horse's instinctive 'programming' to escape. And where his emotional state reaches terror and panic, this is not disobedience: he simply cannot help it.

The standard artificial aids are bits, whips, spurs and training devices such as martingales. The natural aids are those of the body: the voice, seat, weight, hands and legs. Two more very valuable aids, often overlooked, are the eyes and the mind. These are very influential within a close horse-human relationship: horses will almost always go where you look and where you put your weight.

Any signal or sound intended to stimulate a horse to do something can be regarded as an aid – even the flick of an eyelid or a slight lift of a finger.

Horses are *extremely* perceptive of 'body language', a skill that has enabled them to survive for millions of years: it helps them to recognize their herd 'atmosphere', where they stand in the herd hierarchy, and to sense the presence or intentions of predatory animals. Wild and feral *equidae* can tell by a predator's body attitude whether it is hunting or simply passing by.

Teaching aids

We hear a lot today about reward, correction and aids being delivered at the right time because of the short time span available in the horse's brain for him to make the association (within seconds). As far as aids are concerned, the scientific viewpoint today is usually that initially the horse has to perform the movement first, and as soon as the right response becomes habitual, we say the vocal aid as he moves so that he then comes to associate the sound with the movement. For example:

- Fit the horse with a comfortable rope halter that will concentrate pressure more effectively than the usual type of comparatively wide leather or synthetic bands or straps.
- To ask the horse to move forwards, say nothing but exert a steady pull, or intermittent pulls of at least one per second, forwards with the lead rope. The horse realizes fairly quickly that to escape from the pressure (which you must continue) on his poll he must go forwards, away from it.
- The responsibility of the trainer is to release the pressure *immediately*. This stopping of the pressure is the horse's reward. (Some believe it is unlikely that the horse will understand 'good boy' as praise or reward.)
- This technique is repeated several times, and eventually in different locations, until the response becomes a habit and he responds to simply a light pull on the halter. When this is achieved, the vocal aid 'walk on' can accompany the movement so that he links the two.

For more information on this method, see Further Reading on page 151, in particular Dr Paul McGreevy's *Equine Behavior*, Dr Andrew McLean's *The Truth About Horses*, but also Dr Marthe Kiley-Worthington's books *Equine Education* and *Horse Watch*, which give another view.

Once a horse has learned what a specific vocal aid means, it is simple to teach the required movement from the saddle by saying the word, immediately followed by the riding aid.

We are also today much more aware of how easily horses can become confused by being subjected to conflicting aids, such as applying rein and leg aids at the same time. Basically, the young horse learns that a feel on the bit means 'stop' or 'slow' and a squeeze with the legs means 'go'. Looked at this way, it is clear how easily confusion will arise when riders apply both at the same time. It is helpful always to wait a second between the two.

As the horse becomes more expert at dealing with human requests, at least with a competent and empathetic rider, his understanding of, and response to, what we want becomes increasingly refined until ultimately the aids become invisible, horse and rider operating via subtle body position, eyes and mind. This is truly a near-perfect interrelationship, and it is far from impossible.

41 Don't work your horse to exhaustion

In the heat of the moment – an important competition, a productive training session or an exhilarating, active hack – it is easy to miss the signs that your horse is sending you that he is really stressed. Getting a horse fit for his job is an important skill covered in any good book on horse care and management, but there is psychological or mental exhaustion as well as physical, and both of these can ruin your relationship with your horse.

Physical fitness

Any horse has to be made physically fit for his job if he is going to do more than toddle about in walk for an hour. Walking forms the basis of every fitness programme. To get a soft (completely unfit) horse half-fit takes about six weeks.

Start with walking for half an hour a day, then introduce trotting in the third week, and cantering and small jumps in the fifth week. Gradually increase the length of time in each gait until, at the end of the sixth week, you are exercising for about two hours a day, mainly in a smart walk and including, say, three 10-minute spells of trot and two 10-minute spells of canter, including up hills. Larger jumps can now be introduced – but no galloping, even if the horse offers.

The horse is now described as half-fit, a physical state that would be suitable for showing, easy show-jumping or cross-country, half a day's moderate hunting or active hacking, or about 45 minutes of schooling/instruction (with frequent rests). You can take the programme from here.

Temperature, pulse and respiration

The best way to assess your horse's fitness is to measure how quickly his temperature, pulse and respiration return to their normal parameters, see page 129 for how to take these rates. The average rates for a riding horse at rest are:

Temperature: about 38°C or 100.4°F for an average-sized riding horse.
Pulse: about 32 to 42 beats per minute (bpm).
Respiration: about 8 to 16 breaths per minute, in and out counting as one.

After warming up, the **temperature** will rise, but is used as a guide less during moderate work. The **pulse** will be about 60 to 80 bpm. After harder work it will rise, but it should slow down noticeably within 10 minutes, returning to warm-up rate within 20 minutes if the horse is fit for the work you have asked him to do. The **respiration** can reach 100 breaths per minute after fairly taxing work, but again, should be at warm-up rate within 20 minutes. The important point is that *all rates must be back to resting rates within an hour of stopping work*: if not, call a vet.

The results of overwork

Horses become very distressed, both mentally and physically, when they are overworked. Much damage can be done to the horse's body, and the physical stress, even pain, causes psychological distress. Working for too long without enough breaks, even if the horse is physically fit, can embitter any horse and cause behavioural problems associated with psychological distress.

Learn how your horse is feeling by observation, 'feel' and personal study: it is never worth overdoing it, and the horse must always feel able to work easily within himself. Physical fitness, variety and plenty of breaks are the keys.

42 Don't give too many food treats

Food is one of the main things horses live for, particularly grass, the others being comfort, an easy life and company. No wonder we feel that we are being kind to our horses by giving them food treats – anything from lumps of sugar, carrots or apples to commercially produced 'healthy' treats, often low in sugar, full of vitamins and minerals, some also designed to help remove tartar from your horse's teeth.

Why shouldn't I give my horse treats if he enjoys them?

A lot of people find that some horses and ponies become pushy when treats are around. They pester anyone who smells of something delicious, and can even become aggressive if the treats are not forthcoming.

If titbits are given at set times, say after work, this is better than random doling out, but horses know when these are and do expect their treats at that time. Whilst some may just be disappointed if they don't get them, which is unfair and confusing, others can certainly turn quite nasty. None of this is helpful to your relationship.

Training with treats

A popular method of animal training, including with horses, is clicker training. After the horse has done the right thing, the clicker is pressed immediately and tells the horse 'that's right, a treat is coming', and the treat *must* come immediately; the horse then associates the thing he has just done with food, and is inclined to do it again. Once the correct response is being regularly received to the command the treats are no longer required, only the clicker is needed.

Not everyone is in favour of clicker training. Many who appear to be just as successful claim (and I agree) that horses know from the tone of your voice, even with its slight variations, plus your pleased aura, that they have done what you wanted and secured their place in the domestic herd, like pleasing a senior herd member. There isn't even any need to give food, but if you do, make it immediately after the praise so that the horse will link the two.

Titbits are useful to get horses to associate something unpleasant – such as veterinary treatment or clipping – with something tasty, and this has been scientifically proven to make them more amenable at such times.

Does he only want you for what he can get?

It is very common for an owner to give their horse a titbit on arrival at the stable or field, and this is understandable. I prefer the horse to greet me for my own sake rather than for what he can get out of me.

Treats as bribery

Horses surely do not understand the concept of bribery, but titbits can certainly sometimes persuade a horse to go somewhere, or do something about which he is reluctant, provided they are not just used to tease him. When he has done what you wanted, he must have the treat instantly.

43 Understand reward as your horse sees it

This is a very thorny topic. It is most unlikely that horses understand the concept of reward quite as we see it; rather, they simply associate certain tasks, movements or occasions with pleasure created by us, whether it be a titbit, a relaxing stroke, verbal praise or a pleased demeanour. There is even evidence that they understand smiles and laughter, which is not surprising, considering how sensitive they are to moods.

Punishment training

Telling a horse off when he does wrong but *not* praising him when he does right is the same method as the old-fashioned 'punishment training', where human or animal students work to do the right thing – or to not do the wrong thing – so they won't be punished. There is no quicker way to destroy relationships of any kind, to generate lack of respect, dislike and even hatred, or to create actual depression in animal or human.

The sad thing is that many horse owners still operate this way. So many people are quick to reprimand their horses when they do something wrong, or even when they don't do something requested, but are slow to praise them when they do something right. Indeed, some never praise their horses at all, and others do it in a way that the horse does not see either as reward for a specific task or movement, or as pleasure associated with it.

Natural 'rewards'

In a herd, it is unlikely that the members understand reward as we do, as mentioned above, but they do know when they are pleasing or displeasing another horse. Because a cohesive herd provides a strongly knit unit for survival, and nearly all horses want to belong so that they can feel safe, the instinct to get along with, and please others, is strong in horses.

Things that give pleasure are mutual grooming, easy company, mental and physical comfort, being accepted by seniors, and protection if weak or young. Other than a mare suckling her foal, horses do not give each other food treats, nor do they rub each other on the forehead (a current fashion). They do not make sounds to thank or praise others for services rendered, such as flicking flies away from their faces as they stand head to tail, or for moving in a certain way or putting up with something that is uncomfortable or even distressing.

Rewards as we see them

Most people regard titbits and patting as rewarding. Some chatter to their horses for some time after working. Many competitors don't merely pat, but really thump their horses in delight if they have done well. However, the problems with rewards as *we* see them are, variously:

- they are often delivered far too late (the horse cannot link them with what he is being rewarded for);
- the horse does not find them either pleasurable (thumps or even pats) or meaningful (human chatter for no apparent, to him, reason);
- they are often a way of the human releasing their emotions or making themselves feel good because they are doing something they think the horse will appreciate.

Timing

There is no doubt that for pleasure to be connected with an act it has to be done immediately, or within two seconds at the most. Furthermore, with a young, green or 'problem' horse, or one that is new to you, the first thing you must do is be consistent in your treatment of him and behave in a way he understands if you are ever to get through to him and build a good relationship or bond.

Horses are very sensitive to the tones of the human voice, so when he does something right or wanted, you should consistently give a food treat *immediately* if you can (you can't from the saddle), and/or immediately use a word or phrase in a pleased tone that he will come to associate with pleasure on your part, such as 'yes' or 'good boy'. Contrary to some current opinion, this does not have to be said in an identical way each time, though you should try to make it as near the same as you can. Your horse *will* understand the words and your pleased demeanour, and he will link his action with pleasure for him, delivered by a pleased you.

Stroke, don't pat, and definitely don't thump

In natural equine communication, impact sensations, such as kicks, nips and bites, mean displeasure, whereas rubbing, stroking feelings, such as mutual grooming with the teeth and nuzzling with the muzzle, mean pleasure. It is now known that rubbing and stroking a horse around the lower neck and withers area, where horses mutual groom, actually relaxes a horse and lowers his heart rate.

It makes clear sense, therefore, *not* to pat your horse (an impact sensation) and definitely not to thump him (an aggressive impact). Instead, immediately stroke him fairly firmly in the mutual-grooming area to give him pleasure in connection with doing well, and say 'good boy', both easy to do from the saddle. Then he will associate his act with pleasure, and will also know that he has pleased you.

44 Avoid bad ground when possible

Horses' natural underfoot going is turf, ancient grassland with a cushioning mat of roots close up beneath the surface. Equines such as zebras and asses are desert animals: their feet are higher and narrower than horses' to cope with hard, dry ground. Horses' feet are shallower, more open and bigger in relation to the body. They also expand, mainly at the heels, more than those of their desert cousins.

Feet first

The first part of the horse to receive the impact of contact with the ground is the foot, of course. In normal, natural conditions, the foot sinks into the ground a little, which cushions the impact somewhat, the joints of the foot and leg flex, absorbing some more impact, and the tendons are straightened out a little from their normal crimped structure. The muscles in the upper legs (there are none in the lower legs) are stretched because of the pull on the tendons.

The main task of the ligaments is to bind the bones together and stabilize the limbs. In addition, the pads of cartilage between the bones in the joints and their lubricating fluid contribute to the cushioning effect. As the impact is released, the tendons recoil to their normal structure, giving the horse an energy-free boost to his stride, which then begins over again.

Variations from the norm

This system of locomotion works well on the horse's native going, but on stony, frozen, rough or rutted going, slippery ground or in mud, things can go wrong. Uneven, stony or rough ground means that the foot lands unevenly so the force of the impact is not evenly absorbed in the feet and up the leg. If one side of the foot hits the ground first, the whole of that side of the foot and leg receives too much force and the other side receives too little. This can potentially cause compression or crush injuries on the first side, whilst the side can suffer overstretched tissues.

Slippery ground readily causes torn muscles, not only in the legs, as the horse tenses up, slides around and struggles to regain his footing. The suction effect of muddy conditions causes shoes to be pulled off, and may also lead to muscle injuries as the horse is obliged to make above-average muscular effort to free his feet. All bad ground has the potential to cause the horse to stumble or even fall.

What can I do?

Quite simply, avoid bad ground. If you can't, *walk* over it at your horse's chosen speed and give him his head. Sit balanced and still and trust him; he doesn't want to fall any more than you.

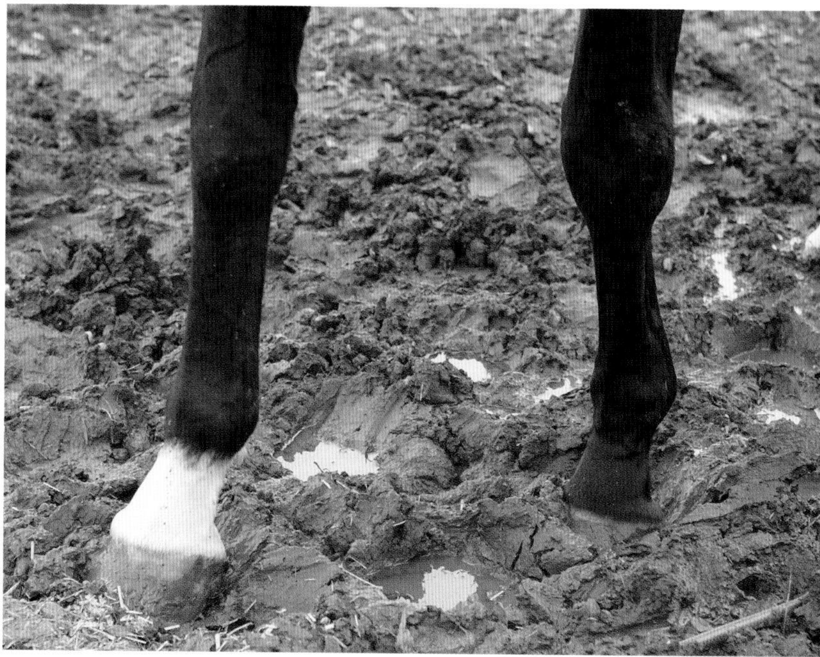

45 Don't work fast or jump on hard ground

Hard ground can mean frozen soil with or without grass on top of it; prepared surfaces that have not lived up to expectations or have worn thin with use and have a hard base; roads and tracks made of tarmac, concrete, paving, asphalt or similar; ground that has been baked hard by the sun; ground that has become hard due to lack of water; and some beaches, notably those with a raised 'crown'.

But horses have worked on hard ground for generations

Even though horses have worked on hard surfaces for a long time, this does not mean that doing so does not harm them. We must remember that horses evolved to run and live on grassland, on turf with an absorbing root mat beneath it. Their legs are brilliantly engineered to absorb a certain amount of concussion through the structure of the joints, ligaments, muscles and tendons: this caters for galloping away from predators on ground that varies in consistency with the seasons. Most of the time, though, they are meant to be on 'giving' ground.

What damage can hard ground do?

The most obvious risk presented by hard ground is that of concussion or jarring. Because the foot hits the ground first, tender feet are a first sign of trouble. The bones inside the feet are attached to the horn wall by means of soft tissues, including the laminae, and concussion can cause tear injuries that may pull apart the tissues and damage blood vessels; this loosens the connection between the bones and the horn wall, causing tenderness and lameness. Otherwise known as concussion laminitis, it may be more or less serious, with all the usual concomitant problems.

Furthermore, on hard ground the joints between the bones are subjected to more impact than they can absorb, and they may also become sore one by one as you go up the leg towards the body.

What can I do?

Do not work at anything faster than a working trot on any hard surface, and certainly do not canter, gallop or jump.

It may be very tempting to attend the last show of a points-accumulator series, or the final championship show, or to 'not let the team down' (often under considerable pressure) by withdrawing due to the ground – or simply to let your horse trot faster than you think is wise or have a spin down a bridleway, but control the urge and don't do it!

Roadwork is a valuable part of any fitness programme, but you would do well to abide by the working trot rule. In fact many people restrict horses' work on hard ground to walking only, and I wouldn't argue with that.

46 Understand and cope with shying

For many riders, shying is quite unnerving: it can be actually unseating, or it can be just a blip in a horse's forward movement. Sometimes we get a warning sign that it is going to happen; at others it comes like lightning out of the blue. It can also, of course, be downright dangerous. But whatever the scenario, it is not appropriate behaviour for a well-mannered horse.

What is a shy?

Sometimes called 'spooking', a shy is a sudden, usually sideways, leap away from something the horse is frightened of. Left to his own devices, he will jump sideways, tense up, turn his head *towards* the monster to look at it and his hindquarters *away* from it. He will snort and make a fuss, but will then often approach to investigate and smell it, and maybe even touch it with his muzzle or a forefoot. As he feels braver, he may want to go round it and examine it from other angles, though not always. After all this he will normally proceed without further ado – unless the rider makes things worse.

Why do shies happen?

Shying is a natural survival mechanism. It can be caused by sounds, such as someone suddenly dropping something near the horse, or starting up a machine – air brakes on a lorry can be very frightening – but more usually it is caused by something the horse has seen and which he thinks is suspect, or has startled him – for instance, a cow behind a hedge suddenly moving.

Because a horse's vision is much more indistinct than ours (see pages 10–11), all that horses see initially is a movement or shape, which can scare them; we, on the other hand, have the advantage of seeing detail clearly and understanding what the object is. Many riders do not appreciate this and punish the horse for being 'silly' or 'naughty', shouting, yanking on the reins, whipping him or kicking him hard. Some people think shying is amusing and do little or nothing to stop it; others try to calm the horse by stroking him and saying 'good boy', which is actually praising him for shying.

So have you actually taught your horse to shy?

Failing to correct and reassure the horse by doing nothing, and also praising him by saying 'good boy' both encourage shying – but punishment actually teaches him to do it. So how can this be?

If a rider punishes a horse straight after he has shied, he will associate the unpleasantness with the object or situation of which he was already frightened, and so is confirmed in his belief that it is dangerous – 'Yes, there is definitely something dangerous around here!' The rider has made the situation much worse and taught him, in one effective, inadvertent lesson, to shy at that spot and at anything else that frightens him in the future.

The more often the rider punishes the horse, the more he will shy because he associates fear or suspicion with abuse and pain following it, and is even more frightened, and it is the rider's fault. Some say that the horse thinks that the object is causing the pain, but I am sure that horses are not so stupid. They know when their riders are hurting them. Probably they are frightened of feeling fear because they know that the rider will hurt them.

What can I do?

Look and think ahead and try to avert the shy by slightly intensifying your outside aids (rein and leg *sideways* against the horse), look ahead (not at the monster) and ride straight.

If the shy starts or happens and you are *not* in a tricky situation such as being in traffic or amongst pedestrians, sit firm, upright and relaxed (leaning forwards weakens your seat) and let the horse approach the monster. Keep in supportive touch with your outside rein and leg, and stroke him with your inside hand on the lower neck and wither, an action that is known to calm horses. Speak firmly and calmly, saying 'easy' or 'all right', *not* 'good boy', which should be reserved for praise. If he starts flying about, control him and gently encourage him with leg aids to approach. Take your time. When he is satisfied it's OK, ride on, and only when you are past it say 'good boy'.

If you can't do this, ride shoulder-in or 'head away', flexed away from the object, and ride positively past it, looking firmly where you want to go and saying 'walk on'. At least turn his head away from it and his quarters towards it, look ahead and try to ride on. For a monster on your left, your aids would be:

- the left rein presses sideways on the neck to turn the shoulders right (but not coming across the withers);
- the right rein feels on the bit as firmly as necessary towards the withers to get right flexion around your right leg, which pushes the horse on. This also has the effect of keeping the quarters left;
- put your weight on your left seat bone and down your left leg (horses usually go where you put your weight);
- try to point with your left hip where you want to go, and look there, too.

In short, it's flex right, go left – and remember to say 'good boy' and stroke him as you succeed.

47 Use an exercise sheet

Some horses and ponies feel the cold more than others, and it is not necessarily always the thin-skinned, 'hot'-blooded breeds, such as Thoroughbreds and Arabs. Some that would not normally feel cold do so when they are clipped, and some simply object to rain. Whatever their particular aversion, it is a kindness, and also sensible, to make sure your horse is comfortable when he is working outside in bad weather.

Does it really make any difference?

If the day is cold but still and dry, few horses will need to wear an exercise or quarter sheet. It is wind and rain, especially together, that intensify the cold. Wind parts the horse's winter coat and destroys the warm air layer next to his skin. It also blows away more quickly the heat always being lost through his skin, so he becomes cold quickly. Moisture is a good conductor of heat, so being wet destroys the coat by (a) flattening it and (b) allowing heat to be lost quickly.

Most horses who are clipped to any great extent and/or have a good deal of 'hot blood' in them will feel the cold in such conditions. Check whether your horse is cold by feeling and looking at him: a cold horse looks hunched up and miserable, and may shiver. Put the flat of your hand on his belly, flanks, loins and quarters, and feel the base of his ears, giving time for heat to come through; then judge honestly. If there is plenty of heat he's probably warm enough, but if he feels lukewarm or chilly he would benefit from a sheet.

When a horse is cold, the blood vessels nearest the skin constrict and so keep more blood deeper inside the body in order to retain heat. The superficial muscles cannot then work well, and injuries, stumbles and falls can occur. Even after warming up, which takes longer in cold weather, a sheet offers protection from wind and rain and is good horse management.

How should a sheet fit?

The muscle-mass areas of the back, loins and hindquarters need protecting from cold so there is little point using a sheet that stops short at the croup. It should come right back to the root of the tail, and there should be a fillet string under the tail to keep the sheet down.

What kind should I use?

To hack out you should perhaps use a high-visibility fluorescent sheet: these are available in three styles – net, waterproof or a warmer, lined version. There are also synthetic and woollen sheets of different weights, and both showerproof and waterproof ones. My favourite is still the yellow, orange and black-striped Witney sheet of fairly thick wool: these sheets are cosy, stay in place well and withstand light rain.

48 Avoid overstressing your horse

It's true that moderate stress is not only good for us, it is also actually beneficial because it stimulates the body's responses to strengthen up against it and to become accustomed to the normal situations that life throws at most of us. Too much, though, is bad for horse and human alike because it maintains our natural flight-or-fight mechanism for sustained periods, which can make the stress levels even worse. Furthermore, if the situation is not relieved it can cause various diseases.

The benefits of allowing time

Many people these days seem to be in a rush – they can't wait to get a young horse working and perhaps competing, or for a horse to overcome injuries and sickness, and they expect their horses to do everything on their owners' terms, whether or not they can.

Rushing the training of young horses is a quick way to ruin them and affect them for the rest of their lives. Putting them into stressful situations before they are mature enough to cope – such as busy showgrounds, long journeys, demanding lessons, frightening traffic and so on – can create lifelong bad memories and behavioural difficulties.

Your attitude to your horse

As far as building up any sort of close partnership or bond with your horse is concerned, it will always be best to put his work and career second to your relationship. Many people buy a horse for a particular job or discipline, but those who are interested in the more spiritual aspects of horse ownership will never let his job interfere with his well-being. Horses and humans can love their jobs, but every living thing needs life balance and to be able to function at a comfortable level.

Riding and over-stress

For the horse, the experience of being ridden can be either stressful or enjoyable. At best it must be somewhat uncomfortable to be tacked up and sat on, to be shod and to be deprived, in the horse's mind at least, of food (especially grass) and water when he wants them. It gets worse when the horse has to put up with thoughtless or domineering riding, or cracking his shins on a jump he had no chance of clearing.

The thing about riding is that we need never stop learning – but it is easy to get into a rut and never ask ourselves if we are really riding as effectively and humanely as we can. As a teacher, I find it particularly common that many riders use a heavy hand contact and nagging legs, rather than aiming at increasing the lightness of aids to the horse's mouth and sides, resulting in self-balance and enjoyment in being ridden for the horse, and in riding for the rider.

For the sake of your partnership, surely it is best to adopt lifelong learning and to constantly aim at improving, but without putting any extra pressure on either yourself or your horse?

49 Give your horse the benefit of the doubt

If we want any degree of success with horses, we have to accept that they do not perceive the world as we do and they do not think as we do. These two facts often result in what, to us, seems like strange behaviour. Although we are both mammals and are thus closely related in the animal kingdom, horses are prey animals with a different mindset from ours; misunderstanding between horse and owner is therefore not uncommon!

Fair play

Many people feel that horses have a sense of fairness, a kind of natural justice. They are quick to assess humans and, having placed us in a certain category – inferior or superior in status, weak, strong, dangerous, safe, reliable, supportive, protective and so on – treat us accordingly, because this is how they operate naturally with other horses and with other animals, and with humans.

I have always found it very noticeable that some horses, usually the most spirited, make it very clear who they want to look after them and who they don't, who they will work for and who they won't, even who they will tolerate near them and who they won't. They have the honesty (although they won't see it like that) to reject or accept people openly, often in an unmistakable way. Not every horse will, or can, get on with every person. We may not be able to see why our horse, for instance, seems to like us but will not put up with a particular groom at the livery yard – but it is as well to respect this. There is obviously a good reason to the horse, and so it should be good enough for us, too.

Empathy and patience

You need to know a horse well to be able to judge why he is behaving in a particular way, but this level of empathy does not have to take a long time. Some horses and people get on well with each other straightaway.

If you are encountering inexplicable behaviour in your horse and you are, at least momentarily, at a loss to understand why, the best course of action is to stand back and consider the situation, meanwhile treating him quietly and positively, not rushing him if he is appearing to find something difficult or unacceptable. Confidently, patiently cajoling a sensitive, spirited horse often works where pushiness and brashness never will.

If your horse develops a 'stop' when jumping, no matter what other people say, and no matter who they are, do not immediately get strong or firm with him. You need to ask yourself:

- Is he stopping at anything and everything? In this case he could either be sickened of jumping, perhaps because he has been overjumped or overfaced, or he is experiencing pain or discomfort.
- Is he stopping at a particular jump or type of jump? In this case check what else is in his area of vision which could be putting him off, or consider whether he needs more practice, and at a lower height, over that type of fence.
- Could he possibly be stopping because your riding technique is hassling him, hurting him, restricting his jumping action, asking him to go too fast or too slowly? All of these can make it impossible for him actually to comply and jump with any degree of safety – and he knows it.
- Could he be stopping because he is afraid due to having hurt himself previously at this particular jump, in this particular spot, over this type of jump, over this colour of jump? In this case think back to his previous experiences, as far as you can.

Position, perform, praise

When working on the flat and asking for, or working on particular movements, remember the classical advice: position the horse so that he can physically move as required, perform the movement (or rather ask, then let him do so), and finally praise him for at least trying or actually succeeding – if you don't praise him immediately he cannot possibly know that he has done what you wanted, so has learnt nothing. If you don't get the movement when you ask for it, ask yourself:

- does he actually understand what you want?
- has your preparation led up to this movement in a logical progression so that he can hardly go wrong?
- are your aids crystal clear, or are you, in your anxiety to get the movement, concentrating on only one part of the aids for the movement and forgetting other aspects? Or are you sitting badly, or putting your weight in the wrong place and so on?

Is correction merited?

If your horse does not do what you have asked, you need to be very certain that he is being 'awkward' before you correct or reprimand him. If you do so and he has not complied because he cannot, your correction may well upset him (you are correcting him for *trying*, which is a serious error on your part). If he misunderstands – almost always the rider's fault due to lack of preparation or clarity – or cannot comply due to pain or physical weakness, say, he may regard your correction or reprimand as confusing and/or unfair, both of which reduce or destroy his trust in you – the last thing you want when trying to create a strong bond with a horse.

50 Never 'saw' your horse's head from side to side

This is a common sight, and the fact that this is sometimes apparently used at the highest levels gives the impression that it is a beneficial practice, so others copy thoughtlessly. I do not believe that this *is* a beneficial practice. At any rate, copying someone without fully understanding why they are doing something can be harmful if the technique is unsuitable for your horse.

Why is this technique ineffective?

The reasons it is usually carried out are:

- to increase flexibility;
- to establish, as a 'reminder', obedience to the rein/bit aids;
- to confirm the control of the rider in the horse's mind.

Done in the way that is usually seen, with the line of the horse's face well behind the vertical and the poll lowered, it could be regarded as domineering, even bullying, and is known from scientific research to prevent the horse seeing ahead because of the structure and functioning of his eyes. None of this speaks to me of a concern for either equine welfare or good horsemanship. In addition, if only the head and neck are flexed, it is achieving nothing in the way of increasing the horse's manoeuvrability. Many of us know that it is quite possible to be carted with the horse's nose on your knee!

What should I do?

To increase flexibility: Perform correct active and passive stretches from the ground, and work the horse in hand (see *Bodywork For Horses* on page 151). In the saddle, concentrate on riding with your seat and accustoming the horse to obeying your weight aids, not merely your hands and legs.

Ridden stretches can help: according to the stage of your horse's schooling, perform your turns by putting your inside seat bone and shoulder forwards into the turn, with your outside leg back from the hip, not just the knee, and looking around your turn. This encourages the horse to flex/bend round your inside leg, gently stretching the muscles on the outside of the circle. Press your outside rein sideways against his neck, and pulse the inside one only as firmly as you need to in order to get the horse to give to the bit in the direction of the circle.

To increase manoeuvrability: To turn a horse quickly and effectively in any gait, press your outside rein firmly sideways against his neck just in front of the withers and feel the inside one intermittently. Put a little weight into your inside stirrup without leaning or tipping over and press your outside leg sideways against his ribs, put your inside seat bone and shoulder forwards into the turn, and look where you want to go. It never fails.

51 Be sure you understand lungeing

Lungeing has been a staple technique in schooling horses for thousands of years. Nearly everyone lunges their horse at some time, often regularly. Lungeing is popular for 'getting the itch out of a horse's heels' before riding, for warming him up, for exercising without carrying weight and, of course, for accustoming a green horse to the weight of a rider whilst still under the control of the trainer.

The rationale behind lungeing

Most standard texts on schooling instruct us that the trainer stands in the centre of a circle and more or less stays there, facing the horse, who circles around the trainer on the end of the lungeing rein. If the trainer stands towards the horse's hip, shoulder or head, these positions are said to, respectively, drive the horse on, slow him down or stop him. Although there is a good basis for this in equine body language or natural communication, it does not happen automatically but has to be taught and emphasized. Usually an assistant leads the horse from the outside of the circle, at least to keep him out on its circumference. It is important that the horse obeys words of command in hand before you start lungeing.

Current thinking concerning lungeing is that it is a form of training which, most of the time, is seen by the horse as being chased away and is, therefore, stressful. Some 'natural' trainers claim that standing square-on to a horse, and certainly behind him or at the hip, is aggressive, which is why the horse moves on.

Common mistakes

The two most common errors in lungeing are to work the horse on much too small a circle, and to ask or allow him to go much too fast in trot and even canter. Both these factors are very likely to strain the horse physically, to spoil his way of going, psychologically to distress him and to adversely affect his view of lungeing and the trainer. None of this is good for your relationship.

What should I do?

To my mind it is preferable to stand slightly sideways-on to most horses, with a soft posture and facial expression, depending on the horse's temperament. Some of the more 'superior' types may need a more controlling attitude and technique, but it is important that you know your horse and act accordingly.

It is also preferable *not* to stand determinedly in the centre of a circle, but to walk in ovals and also straight lines. Small circles should be avoided other than with genuinely advanced and supple horses who can keep their balance on them without undue effort or strain, otherwise the horse can damage his action and gait, not to mention his confidence and trust in you. A lunge rein is plenty long enough, and it's that length for a purpose – to allow the horse to work freely but under control. Let it out to his benefit.

52 Never take out your temper on your horse

I was going to call this topic 'never lose your temper', but there are occasions, however rare, when most of us do lose our tempers, or nearly so. However, people prone to losing their tempers should not be around horses, other animals, children or disadvantaged people who cannot defend themselves – and for horse owners ostensibly wanting to form a special relationship and close partnership with their horse, losing your temper is obviously quite unacceptable.

Anger management

Before considering anger in relation to horses, I should say here that people who know that they tend to lose their temper, even if they feel it is not their fault, need not continue like this. There is a lot of help available, and the place to find it is through a doctor or counsellor.

For some reason, discipline, and especially self-discipline, seems to be a tricky subject these days. In many parts of the world we are familiar with rising levels of antisocial behaviour and violence in our communities. 'Reality' television programmes feature wild, aggressive youngsters and show the remedial treatment for their bad behaviour, the latter being usually the result of inappropriate child skills and lack of discipline at home. At last, though, there are signs of a return to good, basic discipline, self-control and respect for others.

I really hope that this will also reduce the rising levels of cruelty to animals, which is part of the general attitude of some people; that they can do what they like and have their own way. Dogs apparently are the worst affected animals, but in the horse world incidences of ill-treatment can be seen at any equestrian gathering and in many yards. Some riders seem to think that publicly beating up their horse shows not only the horse but also any onlookers that they are strong riders capable of controlling a large, difficult animal. Some regard it as perfectly all right and a normal reaction. How wrong they are.

Discipline or abuse?

As in so many areas of horse care, if we want to produce fairly disciplined and psychologically balanced horses, all we need do is observe what goes on in a herd of horses. Starting as foals with their dams, horses are brought up within definite parameters and are firmly taught to respect their 'betters'. Males in particular will push their luck and try out others to see if they can edge their way up the position ladder, but any horse who messes with a senior is kicked, bitten and driven off in no uncertain terms.

Horse discipline is instant, clear and quick. The horse knows what he is being disciplined for, and what will happen if he tries it again.

When a human rider loses his or her temper with a horse, things are often rather different. Very often the 'discipline' is not understood by the horse because it is the rider's fault. (In my experience, people who lose their temper with their horse are not always good judges of equine behaviour and psychology, or of the principles and techniques of equitation.)

Very often, too, the rider takes too long (many seconds) to administer the discipline, so the horse does not link the 'misbehaviour' with the punishment; for example, the case of an international competitor who whipped his horse about the head as it was walking out of the arena after competing.

Riders who beat up their horses, jab them hard in the mouth and spur them viciously are, of course, plainly abusing and brutalizing their horses. The only time anything approaching violence towards a horse is merited is when the horse is being violent towards you, and you are certain you are not the cause of this behaviour. This does *not* include punishment with bit and spur, because these should only ever be used as communication aids. Some behavioural therapists also think that the whip should not be used either, because it can often escalate into a situation of physical strength (bucking and rearing, or bolting), which the rider cannot handle.

It does take experience to be certain when fair discipline is needed, but I find that it also takes a particular temperament on the part of the rider (calmness and mental clarity, without any need to 'prove' yourself) to do it justly – instantly, clearly and very briefly.

What should I do if I feel I am losing my temper?

Immediately stop what you are doing, and instead briefly do something the horse can easily do well. Praise him genuinely for that, then walk round on a long rein and breathe deeply, thinking of all the good things you can do with your horse! You must make a major effort to finish on a good note before you dismount.

If you are still in a temper, put your horse away (with no rough handling) or ask someone else to do so, then take yourself out of sight and vent your temper on the wall or on a bale of haylage, or use up your energy punching anything that is not alive and therefore capable of being hurt or frightened. Carry on until you are really tired and then, when you are calm, reassess your situation.

53 School on a good surface

Years ago, most 'ordinary' horse owners did not have a manège to work in: you schooled in the best field you could find, on a beach or out on a hack. Indoor schools were definitely the preserve of the superwealthy, of large, important establishments or of military schools.

Why do we need a manège?

We don't actually need one, but an enclosed arena with a good, springy surface is a real boon when schooling. It concentrates the mind of horse and rider, gives a touch of formality to the occasion, even at home ('we're *doing* something'), and feels great to the horse, making his efforts easier and even exhilarating – therefore it's more enjoyable for the rider.

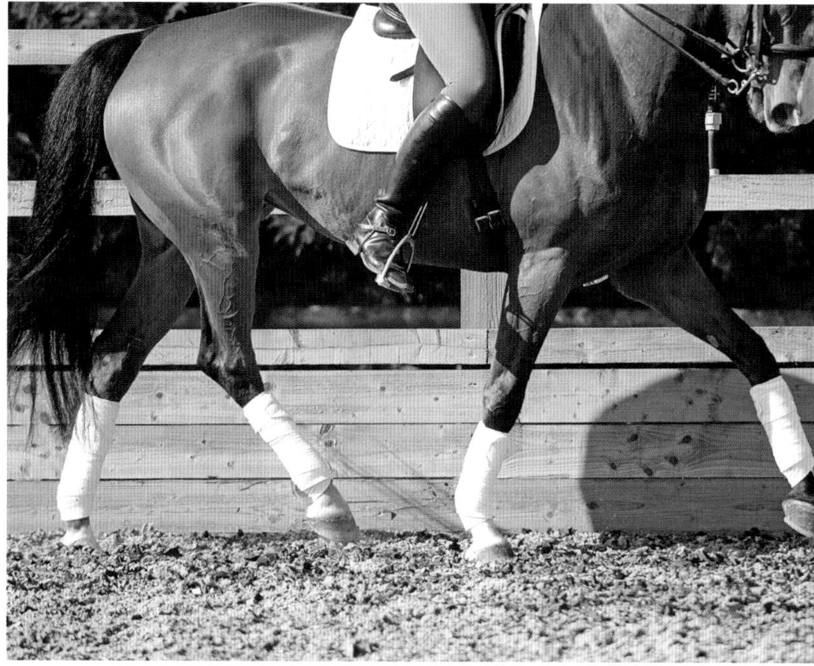

What kind of surface is best?

The lucky few who can school at home on a well-drained and well-maintained lawn surface, sown with football-pitch grasses on a light soil base, have the perfect arrangement because old turf is the sort of going horses are adapted to move on. (See *The Horse Owner's Essential Survival Guide* on page 151 for how to make a good, economy turf or surfaced manège without the need for a membrane.)

For most of us, a stable, synthetic or prepared surface is a desirable alternative, and to merit the description 'good' it must be springy to complement the horse's natural movement. If it is neither too deep nor too shallow, is evenly drained and regularly harrowed, it provides a reliable surface of consistent going, with no nasty surprises such as holes, boggy patches, stones, slippery corners, subsoil or rising membranes.

Sand alone is not good enough, although it is often used because it is cheap. It is absolutely dead going (no spring at all), holds the water, becomes deep when very damp and slides around when dry if too much is used, as is often the case. Sand well mixed with rubber, however, is a great improvement if it is not too deep and kept well harrowed.

Ordinary, large woodchips wear badly and can be slippery, but finer wood shreds are springy and very stable, and if such a surface is used for only a very few horses, it barely needs harrowing, if at all.

There are new surfaces coming out all the time, and plenty of firms are willing to revamp old arenas or install all or a part of new ones, with a wide range of prices. Remember the above criteria when giving your specifications and getting quotes.

54 When jumping, don't overface your horse

It is not always easy to strike a good balance between the abilities and preferences of horse and rider when it comes to jumping. Jumping is all about confidence – that is, confidence of both horse and rider. Although schoolmaster jumpers may be ideal to help along a less confident rider, a very confident rider can easily ask too much of a horse, and this often ruins the horse's trust.

It's all a matter of judgement

Judgement is a crucial skill for training horses well. Some people have it naturally, but it can be learned, and you need it if you want to create an enthusiastic, safe, sensible jumper who enjoys his work and does not put both of you at any more risk than is already inherent in the activity.

Judgement can be acquired by means of studying your sport, your horse and your technique with a really good teacher, and studying as many jumpers as you can through their body language and attitudes. Watch the riders' techniques, and their horses' reactions, thoughtfully and start judging others at every level.

Many horses jump badly or start disliking jumping because their riders restrict them due to:

- lack of control as a direct result of inadequate schooling on the flat;
- lack of an independent, balanced seat over fences, which leads to their using the reins and the horse's neck to balance and stay 'with' the movement;
- ill-treatment during jumping.

How can I tell if I am overfacing my horse?

To overface a horse means to ask him to jump beyond his abilities – jumps that are too high, too wide, too many, too often or too difficult. Jumping when unfit, injured or tired are also causes. An overfaced horse usually gives you a feeling of 'back-pedalling' or of swerving from side to side or to one side. Another sign is rushing fences: rushing is *not always* a sign of keenness. If you miss these signs the horse could start refusing, running out and napping near jumps.

Provided you are absolutely certain that you yourself have no fear of the fence, are riding in such a way as to help and not hinder him and are presenting him correctly, calmly and confidently, you can be sure that your horse has a confidence problem: that is, you are overfacing him.

How often should I jump my horse?

When he is jumping small fences you can pop a few on most days for five or ten minutes. As his ability and the height of the jumps increase, restrict it to a couple of times a week, if that. Many jumpers at higher levels rarely jump except in competition. Take little obstacles out hacking, too.

55 Don't work your horse behind the vertical

It is amazing how quickly fashions 'catch hold' in the horse world. Sadly for horses, a current fashion is to work them 'behind the vertical' – with the front of their face behind a vertical line dropped straight down to the ground – and this practice has become widespread. Because many riders in top levels of competition do it, others understandably think that it is the thing to do and copy them, without having the knowledge to judge whether it is really beneficial.

A telling comparison

I recently returned home from a display of equitation, classical and other types, and during the whole of the programme, involving several different breeds and types of horse and superbly skilled riders, not one horse was ever presented working behind the vertical. Many worked in self-carriage with no rein pressure and with either a loose noseband or none at all. The horses were fit, often highly collected, obviously very light in hand, beautifully balanced, extremely agile and spirited, but calm, self-controlled, instantly responsive to the lightest aids and completely on top of their job.

What a different sight from much of the riding we often see elsewhere, where so often horses work (or rather struggle) behind – sometimes well behind – the vertical, with a shortened, compressed neck due to harsh rein contact and a tight noseband. Many are anxious and in a real sweat, with raised blood vessels, splashed with froth, eyes often wide and distressed, stiff in the back and neck in every gait, with unnaturally exaggerated movement and a distorted posture in their overall performances; their whole demeanour presents a most upsetting picture to a knowledgeable horse lover.

It must be clear to any concerned horse owner that putting a horse into such a state cannot give him any enjoyment in his work or pleasure in the company of the person who causes such obvious psychological distress and physical discomfort. Surely a rider willing to do that to a horse cannot regard his well-being and welfare as being of paramount concern.

Consulting the real experts

Any of the most revered and respected standard texts on schooling horses, from previous centuries up to and including the present day, when we have increased knowledge of physiology, will confirm that during schooling or performance, the horse's poll must be the highest point of the neck (although some allowances are made for stallions with crested necks), and the front of the face must be in front of the vertical line when the head is viewed from the side. These requirements are also clearly stated in the rules of the FEI (Fédération Équestre Internationale), which governs equestrian competitive sports worldwide.

Words and expressions that are used in some of the texts mentioned above to describe this faulty way of going, its causes and adverse consequences, include:

- an enforced and incorrect form of collection;
- an artificially shortened neck, a tight back, and as a result, imperfect hindquarter engagement;
- a serious defective position of the head;
- a potentially physically injurious head position;
- incompetence of the rider;
- inadequate horsemanship skills;
- ugly and abusive;

and many more in the same vein.

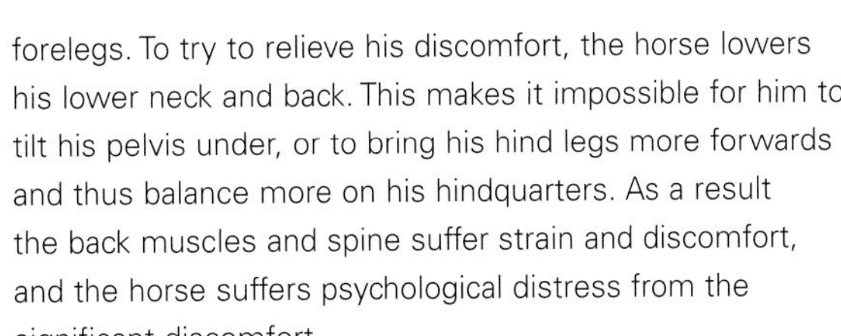

Studying the way a horse should go in any of those books (see page 151, in particular *100 Ways To Improve Your Riding* and *100 Ways To Improve Your Horse's Schooling*) will make clear in minutes how a horse should go; that is: when asked to collect, the horse should carry himself with his neck arched but reaching *forwards*, with the poll the highest point and the front of the face just in front of the vertical.

The horse rounds his back upwards, and the pelvis and hind legs are tilted under and brought more forwards; this enables him to put more weight on his hindquarters and become light in hand with a comfortable, swinging back and free forward movement – and this controlled freedom is what every good horseman and woman should be aiming for.

The basic consequences of enforced, incorrect action and posture

Equine bodywork therapists are well aware of the consequences of the type of riding and way of going that is probable when the horse's head is behind the vertical.

The common results of having the muzzle pulled in and back and the neck artificially rounded and/or shortened, usually with the poll low and the chin approaching, or actually on, the chest, are stressed and strained muscles and soft tissues in the neck, shoulders, chest and upper forelegs. To try to relieve his discomfort, the horse lowers his lower neck and back. This makes it impossible for him to tilt his pelvis under, or to bring his hind legs more forwards and thus balance more on his hindquarters. As a result the back muscles and spine suffer strain and discomfort, and the horse suffers psychological distress from the significant discomfort.

What modern equine science tells us

Recent scientific research has made it clear that, because of the structure and functioning of the horse's eyes, he cannot see ahead when his head is in this behind-the-vertical or even on-the-vertical posture, only down at the ground. Therefore, in addition to the psychological distress of the physical discomfort, he also experiences the insecurity and anxiety of not being able to see where he is going.

What can I do?

Do not ride your horse in the way described, no matter who you see doing so, or who tells you to do it. Read and learn all you can from reliable books (see page151), and seek out other teachers and question them before booking a lesson. In addition, re-read page 12.

56 Limit work on circles

A common sight on most yards is that of horses being lunged or ridden round and round on circles, usually at trot, as if straight lines were not allowed. And very often these circles are too small. A 10m (33ft) circle, for instance, is regarded as quite a difficult movement under saddle, and can certainly be harmful on the lunge, as shown by horses flying about with their shoulders leading and quarters out.

But my horse needs to learn to bend and flex

Bending and flexing are of course an important part of the horse's training, and circles and especially turns (which are only parts of circles, so are not as demanding) are valuable for this; however, circles can be quite stressful to a horse, and should be used only with discretion.

On a circle, your horse is asked to bend or flex so that he conforms approximately to the circle. I say 'approximately' because we have known for years that the horse's spine, made up of little bones called vertebrae that are protected by pads of gristle (cartilage) between them, has only a little lateral flexibility, and the concept of its following exactly the line of the circle, at least a smallish one, is in practice impossible.

The horse must readily flex longitudinally (along the length of his body), arching his spine from croup to poll into what we term a 'vertebral bow' (see page 151, in particular *100 Ways To Improve Your Riding* and *100 Ways To Improve Your Horse's Schooling*).

Before he can perform good lateral flexions the horse has to bring his hindquarters and legs underneath his body, thus lifting his back and shifting more weight on to the quarters. This lightens the forehand so that he can more easily bring his forefeet very slightly across in front of his hind feet in the direction of the circle. There is no other way he can turn as we require, especially on smallish circles, because of the lack of lateral flexibility in his spine.

This is why circles are more difficult and demanding than straight lines. They are clearly quite a gymnastic effort, which also puts extra stress on the joints of the inside legs because these take more weight from the feet all the way up to the hips and shoulders – not to mention his muscles, which he is using to balance his body around the circle. Too much work on circles is therefore not going to do your horse any favours.

What can I do?

To relieve his mind and body of some of this stress, start with parts of circles, and do large ones of at least 20m (66ft) at first until your horse can balance well on them. Do plenty of work on straight lines and make your turns wide and shallow, not going deep into the corners. Use shallow loops, too, and give your horse plenty of breaks on a free rein.

57 Learn long-reining from an expert

Long-reining justifiably has the reputation of being more versatile than lungeing. You can change direction more easily, and if you have the skill, can school the horse up to high standards, including High School, on long-reins. The down side is that it is harder on the trainer if he or she is not particularly young, fit or agile because of the need to go just as far and fast as the horse, which often means doing it at the run!

Some points about long-reining

Before a horse is introduced to long-reins he should be well established in lungeing and wearing a saddle and bridle, and must be readily obedient to vocal aids. He needs to carry himself well, to flex longitudinally and laterally, to accept the bit and respond to light rein aids.

Needless to say, he must not be afraid of the whip or of the reins touching his body. He will have become used to watching the whip during lungeing, but you now have to gradually accustom him to the reins. Get someone competent and calm to hold him whilst you confidently but carefully rub the reins on his body, including his back and hind legs, until he makes not the slightest objection.

Many trainers also use side-reins for long-reining, which must be adjusted so that they only come into play if the horse plays about. Their object is *not* to force the head carriage – this is most important. You can attach them to a roller or the girth straps of your saddle.

Finding a trainer

Most classical trainers will be happy to teach you to long-rein, and you should be able to find a trainer through the Classical Riding Club (see page 152). You may discover a local trainer through other owners or a good riding centre. Make contact by phone or e-mail, or visit them and explain what you want. You will find learning from an expert who is sympathetic to both you and your horse safer and much more enlightening than risking a fiasco on your own if you are new to the art.

What to expect

A good trainer will spend a little time getting to know your horse, and will probably first lunge him to check his responses. He or she will show you how to fit the equipment, and will answer any queries you have. You may be needed to walk at your horse's head at first until he understands this new technique. When he becomes confident at it – and how long this takes will vary with each horse – the trainer will hand over the reins to you and go with you, instructing you as you learn this valuable new skill.

Most horses enjoy long-reining. It forms an extra groundwork activity for them, and gets *you* fit as well!

58 Learn a soft sitting trot

Once you have learned how to do a sitting trot that absorbs the movements of your horse's back, you may be surprised by how much easier it is to go with him and to school him, and how much more enjoyment he finds in his work. You will also start noticing how badly many people perform sitting trot! Having a rider repeatedly thudding down on his back over long periods must be a horrible experience for any horse.

First learn to relax

It is impossible to do a correct, soft sitting trot if your body is rigid. The horse's back moves up and down and from side to side with each step, and your body from the waist down must absorb and go with these movements as though it is part of the horse.

Some people are stiff because they are trying too hard, which always creates tension; others are not naturally supple and co-ordinated. In my experience, however, it is only a very few people who cannot learn to do an acceptable sitting trot using the techniques below.

Start relaxing in walk

Enlist the help of a sensible friend to lead your horse. Sit in the saddle without stirrups and with a completely free rein held at the buckle. Feel your seat bones directly under your body and sit lightly on them, not your buttocks. Gently stretch your upper body and head upwards from the waist, with the shoulders back and down and the chest up a little. If you now find that you tend to hollow your back, push your spine slightly back into the waistband of your jodhpurs and hold your upper body gently in this toned, upright position, looking ahead.

Now, completely loosen the muscles of your buttocks and legs, with the toes dropped – not pushed – down, so that your friend can lift your legs sideways away from your horse and they just flop back lifelessly. This total relaxation of the lower body is essential to learning to feel.

Walk on, stretching up from the waist and dropping down from the waist, letting your legs swing and your seat feel the rhythmic movements of your horse's back. It's much easier to *feel* if you look ahead and not down at your horse, so tell your friend to keep reminding you of this. Keep your upper body out of it by stretching gently up, chest up, shoulders back, down and *still*, not swinging with your seat. All the movement is absorbed below your waist.

Now try jogging

Put your horse into a jog or *slow* trot and keep the same posture – stretch up from the waist, drop down from the waist and look ahead. Keep your seat and legs loose and floppy, and lean back slightly. *If you lean forwards at this stage you will never master it, and you won't if your horse trots fast, either.*

Now imagine that your seat and thighs are gently glued to your saddle and have to move with it. What happens when you 'stick' with the movement like this is that the base of your pelvis (seat bones and pubic bone) alternately tilts forward and up, and back and down, as your horse, respectively, rises and lands in trot. Also, the small of your back alternately flattens and hollows as his back rises (in the moment of suspension) and drops (as he lands).

So, when he rises you take up his back under your seat by tilting the bottom of your pelvis forwards and up, which flattens the small of your own back a little. When he lands you allow your pelvis to tilt down softly again, which slightly hollows the small of your back. This is the 'pelvic tilt' familiar to dancers, gymnasts and yoga and Pilates enthusiasts. Keep your upper body proud and still, looking ahead, your lower body completely loose and 'following', and lean back very slightly in a sort of 'Red Indian' trot. You may find that your seat also follows the sideways swing of the back up and down if you are really loose.

Don't try too hard, as this will tense you up. If you master this technique, you will avoid two very common, ugly and damaging errors in sitting trot (apart from thudding): nodding the head, and moving the hands up and down with the horse's rise and fall. Even with a loose rein the horse can feel this, but if you do it with anything like a contact it is extremely unpleasant for him and will affect both his action and his mental attitude towards being ridden.

Do not be ashamed of holding the pommel of your saddle lightly as you learn this technique. Many people used to gripping with stiff legs need a little help balancing when their legs and seat are properly loose, and holding on is fine.

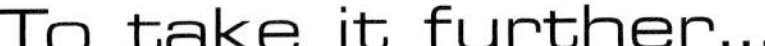

To take it further...

The next stage is to ask for a *slightly* more energetic trot, and after that to take back your stirrups, which you'll probably need to make longer. Ultimately you will acquire the knack of letting your legs drop down through your heels, and of giving leg aids and just keeping your legs in and 'toned' without pressing them against your horse all the time, which is counterproductive to true lightness of the sides and is betrayed by bare patches on the horse's sides, where the rider's legs lie.

59 Create a multi-discipline horse!

Horses are much more adaptable than most humans, and it is in fact we who categorize them as horses for certain disciplines: the dressage horse, the show jumper, the eventer, the hunter, the racehorse and so on. Many horses these days are clearly bored with their lives, particularly those that are kept to one job and hardly ever, or never, turned out with their friends. Don't let this happen to yours.

Compile an equine CV for your horse

One evening when you haven't much to do, sit down at your PC or equip yourself with a pen and paper, and work out a *curriculum vitae* for your horse, as if he were applying for a job. Make out this CV not necessarily on what he has achieved, but on his personality, temperament and skills, both on the ground, in his off-duty time and under saddle, or in harness if you drive; and then work out what other disciplines those qualities could be used for.

Keep positive, but be realistic. First list all his good points, then list his moderate points, and finally his bad ones if he has any, including any health issues that could hinder him, such as a wind problem (no fast work) or weak hocks (can't jump).

Imagine that your horse has a superbly quiet and affectionate temperament and is a patent safety ride. I'll bet you know several nervous riders who would love to meet him and have a little ride: they and he will both make a new friend, he will have added interest and will help someone regain their nerve. He may even be able to help with Riding for the Disabled.

If he is a terrific jumper but you only ever show-jump, take him hunting, hunter-trialling or team-chasing for a change. If you can get a passable dressage test out of him, you could also event. You could work out some active hacks and farm or park rides that involve jumps.

Dressage horses often lead excessively restricted lives. Think laterally and do some showing as well, and be adventurous in your classes – for example, if your horse is getting on a bit take him in veteran classes; if he is beautifully behaved try 'family horse' classes or local pageants or displays. Equitation classes, fancy dress classes, pairs and teams, if you can find them, can all add variety to both your lives.

If you know that your show or dressage horse can jump but *you* don't want to, let someone else who is a competent jumping rider develop this side of his life. Maybe you could do them a good turn by, perhaps, schooling their horse on the flat.

60 Get yourself fit and supple

First the bad news: riding alone is not enough to get you fit. Now the good news: getting supple and fit benefits every other area of your life. People who are naturally active or even athletic will find that a certain amount of structured activity is no trouble – but the less energetic amongst us will fear that it sounds like torture and is *so* time-consuming. But the secret is never to overdo it, and to start gently.

Why do I have to be fit? My horse does all the work!

It's important that you look after your *own* fitness, too. Riding *is* exercise, and you must be aware of feeling at least a little different after you dismount – some people are either fairly, or very, tired, whereas others feel more of a mental and physical buzz. And the reason you need to be fit, strong and supple is so that you can ride properly and help your horse. For the horse, there must be nothing worse than having a big, unbalanced, top-heavy 'sack of potatoes' flopping and swinging around on his back, because as well as trying to do what the sack is asking, he also has to balance himself and counteract its influences. This makes being ridden three times more difficult than it need be, and much less enjoyable.

What can I do?

If you look after your own horse you will have a moderate degree of heart and lung fitness, but some extra brisk walking or cycling, with a few hills included en route, will stimulate your heart and lungs to work more, as will dancing, swimming or any other active sport. Try the usual advice of walking upstairs instead of taking the lift, getting off the bus a stop earlier, walking to and from the shops and so on.

Strength can come from careful work with weights and various exercise machines at home or in a gym. Pilates also strengthens the body, and yoga greatly increases suppleness. Some horse magazines and books on riding include exercises for riders. Standing on a step on the balls of your feet and letting your weight drop down through your heels stretches the backs of your legs, and the exercise involving careful sideways leg lifts stretches the tissues down the insides of your legs and opens your hips so that you can sit in your saddle, rather than on it, and get your legs round your horse.

If you think you need expert advice you can join your local gym: explain to the coach what is involved in your sport, and request that a personalized exercise programme be worked out for you. You don't need to do this extra exercise every day: two or three days a week should do it, and you're sure to feel better for it.

61 A meticulous fitness and schooling plan

Fitness and schooling are two important parts of your horse's life that need careful planning if he is to do anything more than very light work. Schooling can create fitness, but it can be more demanding than many realize. Knowing your horse's capabilities at any particular time is important in not overstressing him from the viewpoint of athletic effort and the difficulty of schooling exercises.

Where do I start with a fitness programme?

Start by re-reading page 66 for basic information on getting a horse fit, and see page 151, in particular *100 Ways To Improve Your Horse's Health* and *The Horse Owner's Essential Survival Guide*.

First of all, take your horse's temperature, pulse and respiration (TPR) rates at rest at the same time and under the same quiet conditions every day for about a week, so that you get to know his normal at-rest rates. Then start taking the pulse and respiration regularly after warming up, immediately after work, 20 minutes after that, and an hour after stopping work, when you should also check his temperature. This will give you a very clear idea of how fit he is, and so at what point to start your programme.

Remember:

- It takes 6 weeks to get a completely soft, unfit horse half fit.
- It takes 9 or 10 weeks to get him fit for most ordinary riding club and local show competitions.
- It takes 10 or 12 weeks to get him fit to start eventing, or to do lower-level endurance rides and pursuits requiring that sort of fitness.
- It takes about 16 weeks to get a horse fit for almost anything – a level unlikely to be needed by most amateur owners' horses.

Remember to plan your horse's feeding along with his exercise schedule. This is a very individual thing, and ideas about it have changed in recent years. Most horses do not need anything like the amount of cereals we previously thought they did, because of the availability of high-energy fibre and other feeds. A good plan is to ring the helpline at the company whose feeds you use, and discuss your intentions with one of their qualified nutritionists.

Any fitness and feeding programme needs to be flexible, so allow a couple of extra weeks to cater for lay-offs due to sickness or injury. To fit your schedule into your year you could try the following:

- Assess the level of fitness required for the first demanding occasion that you plan for you and your horse, whether it is a competition, an organized pleasure ride, a holiday with your horse, or an active hack with friends. You will find this information in the books recommended (see page 151), or in any good book on equine fitness or care.
- Take into account your horse's present level of fitness.
- Deduct the number of weeks it would take to go from unfit to his present level, from the total number of weeks needed to reach the required level.
- Count that number of weeks backwards from your first 'event', add your two contingency weeks and start the programme then, or before.

Where do I start with a schooling programme?

Programmes of progression in schooling for both basic flatwork (from walking on straight lines to walk-to-canter) and basic lateral work (from turn on or about the forehand, to shoulder-out or counter shoulder-in) are given in *100 Ways to Improve Your Horse's Schooling*. It is difficult to give a schooling programme in terms of time, however, as everything depends on the skill of the trainer and the 'trainability' and past experiences of the horse.

It is easier to school a horse from completely 'green' because he will have no previous bad experiences and will not have been taught according to any method that is different from yours. A horse with a little experience, such as one that is 'backed and ready to ride away' or is even 'backed and going nicely', may in fact have been schooled in a way that is quite different from your own and your trainer's beliefs and techniques, and may have a number of hidden (and therefore undeclared) problems that will have to be overcome, at the same time as you are trying to make progress with him.

However, a green horse and a novice rider can be an extremely risky combination. Unlike buying a puppy, it is not like 'growing up together' with horses: they are potentially dangerous flight animals that need knowledgeable handling, especially when unschooled. The best way, used by all the best, most skilful and empathetic trainers and major riding academies of the world, is for the best and most experienced riders to school the green (novice) horses, and the made (fully schooled) horses to teach the novice, or poor, riders.

The better the trainer and the more of a 'clean sheet' that you have with your horse, the quicker your progress will be. A 'problem' horse and a novice owner may be struggling a year and more later if they are still alive and together, but a green horse and a skilful trainer can be walking, trotting and cantering in good balance on straight lines and circles, and negotiating single poles on the ground with no fuss, in six months.

Health and management

It's all up to you

Whatever you do with your horse in the way of work, performance or competition, there is no denying that his efforts are largely determined by the care he receives in the stable or field. No horse who is not healthy, comfortable, secure in himself and contented will be able to do his best under saddle, in harness or working in hand, no matter how well schooled he is or how willing he feels. Health and well-being, both mental and physical, are everything, and any veterinary surgeon or other health professional will tell you that good health mainly depends on the care the horse receives and the lifestyle and surroundings he experiences when he is at home.

I have always found horse care and management fascinating and extremely rewarding, but it is essential to observe constantly the following two rules if you want to ensure that your horses have the best of care at any time:

- To study and get to know horses really well, especially – but not just – your own.
- To keep up to date with the latest information on veterinary and management science.

The successful blending of the two is the way to ensure that your horse always receives the very best of care. Some older books on horses are excellent, but equine research moves on, often quite quickly, and new veterinary techniques and medicines, and improved knowledge of nutrition, behaviour, fitness and so on, become available to us, to the advantage and benefit of our horses.

Horse magazines and books on technical, how-to-do-it subjects go out of date fairly quickly, and any veterinary book that is five and certainly ten years old should be replaced with its newer, revised edition, or with a newer book. It is important to check in the front of the book when it was *revised*, and not just reprinted. A new or revised edition will contain the latest thinking and information.

There are some wonderful older books, classics of their type, which never seem to be superseded. This is particularly so in the field of equitation, because nowadays a much harder (on the horse) style of riding seems to prevail than in previous generations, and this can create welfare issues and problems of well-being not always recognized by owners. The only major improvements here are in the sciences of equine behaviour, training/learning psychology and biodynamics – the way horses move. Certainly the advances in these fields will help the humane working and schooling of horses to proliferate, *if* these methods are applied in practice. It is the responsibility of owners, managers and trainers to keep up to date.

Just as confusing training and hard riding techniques will undoubtedly affect a horse's physical comfort and soundness, his psychological contentment and, consequently, his general well-being, so indeed will poor care.

You really cannot separate management and work.

62 Think 'prevent' rather than 'cure'

The truth is that vets' bills are expensive, and so are insurance premiums. We all need to call in the vet or some other type of health specialist at times for sickness, injury or routine health maintenance such as vaccinations – but none of us wants to do so any more than is necessary. The main reason for working to prevent problems is, of course, our horses' welfare – and there is a lot we can do in this regard.

Work judiciously

People who care about their horses do not work them, competitively or otherwise, in conditions that put them at unnecessary risk. This might include jumping on hard ground, doing fast work on uneven, deep or stony ground, working them to the point of distress or in tack that causes discomfort or pain, or when they have an injury that work will exacerbate, or when they have not sufficiently recovered from injury, and so on.

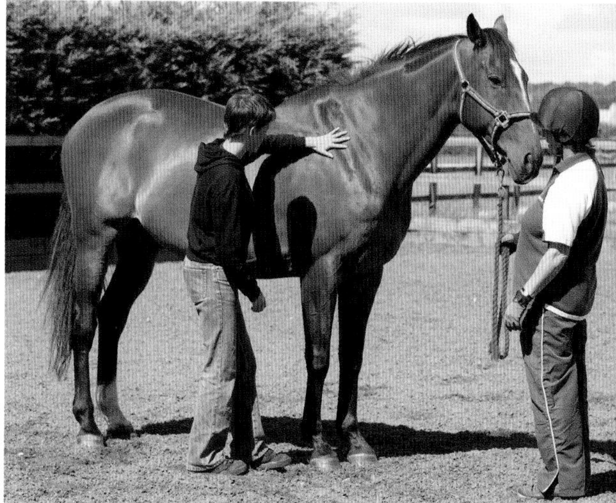

Preventive care

- One of the most effective ways to keep a horse in good health is to keep him correctly nourished. An appropriate diet goes a long way towards giving him the physical strength to avoid injury, stimulating his immune system to protect him from disease and supplying his body with the materials it needs to enable it to maintain itself in optimum health. Ample, clean water is his most important nutrient.
- Keeping a horse properly fit for his work keeps him healthier, as well as able to work. Suitable schooling exercises and ridden work aimed at carefully taxing all parts of his physique, whatever his job, create all-round, balanced strength and development.
- Owners can do a lot to improve their horses' health and comfort by careful and thorough grooming, hand rubbing and basic massage, including stretches.
- Good farriery, carried out often enough, keeps a horse comfortable on his feet and able to move with safety and agility. Uncomfortable feet cause awkward and unnatural movement, which stresses other tissues, develops the 'wrong' muscles, and mentally distresses the horse.
- Several hours of freedom on most days with friends is a horse's means of recreation and relaxation, both of which are necessary to his contentment.
- Keeping his bed adequately thick, clean and dry so he can stale and lie down in comfort is important but is often neglected. Horses cannot lie down in comfort on insufficient bedding, and dirty floors and bedding that is damp with urine give off ammonia, which damages hoof horn and the respiratory tract.
- Shelter and appropriate clothing when necessary help to provide protection from debilitating weather and insects.

These are just some of the most obvious management factors that can (a) prevent problems, and (b) enhance your horse's resistance and comfort, making injury, illness and treatment less likely.

63 Check local weather forecasts

What's the point of checking the weather forecasts? Of course you can't do anything about the weather, *but* you can do a lot to protect yourself and your horse from the worst of it by timing your outdoor work spells; furthermore, not only can you then be sure you are wearing protective clothing, but you will be better aware of what the weather will do to ground conditions at that particular time of year. You can also help outdoor horses more if you are forewarned.

Weather forecasts

In addition to national and regional television and radio stations, the Internet gives localized forecasts, and you can have them sent to your mobile phone by various means. Just about every newspaper gives them, too.

If you live near the coast, you can check your local tide tables if you are planning to arrange a beach ride; these tables will also be given in your local paper, and a list should be available from your local council by e-mail and maybe on its website.

Most owners who have to go away to their workplace are familiar with the scenario of looking out of the window at the weather and wondering if their horse is all right. It is a frustrating situation, especially in the UK and Ireland, where the vagaries of the weather are such that we often experience all four seasons in one day; very often it is difficult to decide what to do before setting off for work – whether to turn the horse out, leave him in, rug him up or not rug him up.

Checking the local weather forecast the previous evening should alleviate your stress levels because you can rug up, or not, accordingly. In doubtful weather, rely on light- to medium-weight rugs and sheets so that your horse has good protection from wet and cold but will not be overrugged. Ensuring that your turnout areas have adequate shelter will also save you worry.

From spring to autumn, insect sheets may be standard turnout wear for some horses and ponies – and if the forecast is for a hot sunny day, it may well be better to leave your horse in a well-ventilated stable with hay, water and a good bed, and turn him out at night instead.

Riding out in most weathers

If you can vary the timing of your ride, checking the local forecast can help you decide when to set out – for instance, you could choose to avoid a rainy morning and ride in the afternoon instead. A light waterproof exercise sheet is a good idea for your horse; these sheets are also windproof because of the nature of their fabric. The traditional woollen exercise sheets are both warm and showerproof.

In wet and really cold weather, it's best to ride out in a proper riding coat that will cover your thighs, not the fashionable bomber-jacket type that stops at your hips and is not much use in such weather.

64 Learn body-brushing and wisping as therapy

Grooming is a very important part of good horse care, but it is often not well understood these days and is rarely done properly. It is also tempting to skimp on it because of lack of time, or to simply wash the horse down occasionally to remove mud and dirt. However, proper body-brushing is a mini-massage in itself, which your horse could enjoy most days. And have you never heard of wisping? You very soon will!

Body-brushing

Body-brushing is hard work if you do it properly, but it has definite advantages:

- it gets you fit and strong (always a good idea);
- it benefits your horse by massaging his superficial muscles,
- stimulating the circulation in his skin and muscles, and
- cleaning his skin and coat.

Buy yourself a high quality, natural-bristle body brush or two with a hand loop across the back, obtainable mainly from traditional saddlers such as W. H. Gidden in London (see page 152), who will order things for you and will sell by mail order. These work far better than synthetic ones because they really clean the coat and skin and smooth and shine the hair. Synthetic brushes can scratch and dull the coat, and some create static electricity that raises the hair and attracts dust, none of which you want.

Body-brushing comes after you have removed the main dirt with the dandy brush. Brush the head, including both the inside and the outside of the ears, firmly but considerately. Clean the brush every few strokes by pulling the bristles, facing downwards, across the teeth of the metal curry comb, which you tap on its side occasionally to dislodge grease and dandruff.

Then brush the whole horse from just behind the head, working down and back with the hair. Stand a little away from the horse on, say, his left (near) side, brush in your left hand, curry in your right. With your left arm rather stiff and your elbow bent, place the brush on the coat and lean your weight on to the horse, pushing the bristles through to the skin (which is the whole idea) in a long, smooth, firm stroke (see opposite). Pick up the brush and repeat, doing about six strokes in one place. Clean the brush every two or three strokes. Go all over the body like this. Of course, you have to modify your technique on the legs, and be careful not to knock bony areas such as the head, hips and so on.

The areas usually forgotten or skimped are inside the ears, under the forelock, mane and tail, between the jawbones, behind the elbows, the underneath of the horse, between the hindlegs and behind the pasterns.

Wisping

Wisping is a form of 'do-it-yourself' massage that any owner can learn. It is done after body-brushing to further lubricate the skin and coat with natural oils, to stimulate the skin, and to treat muscles after work (like an athlete's rub-down and massage), loosening them up, relaxing them, and enhancing the blood flow through them.

Wisping is done with a pad made from a twisted 'rope' of hay or haylage. You can buy stuffed massage pads of chamois or fabric but they are not so good – and why spend money when you can make them. Firmly but carefully bang the wisp down (which is why it is sometimes called 'banging') on the horse's muscle-mass areas – and *only* on these.

Stand as for body-brushing, and firmly but carefully bang the flat of the wisp down with your bodyweight on to the muscles, then press it along with the direction of the hair; lift and repeat, doing about three to six rhythmic 'bangs' and strokes in one area. Ideally the horse should flinch his muscles anticipating the slap, which contracts and develops them, then the pressure relaxes them and alternately flattens and releases the blood vessels, pumping blood through the muscles – a very therapeutic exercise.

Grooming and wisping combined are a restorative finish to a taxing exercise or work period. Stabled horses should be fully groomed daily or on most days, and wisped on several days a week. A full grooming followed by wisping will take an experienced groom about an hour. Treat these tasks as a therapeutic and relaxing treat for your horse. Don't rush them, do them rhythmically, and let your horse eat his hay as you work. This is real 'together' time! Get right down to the skin at

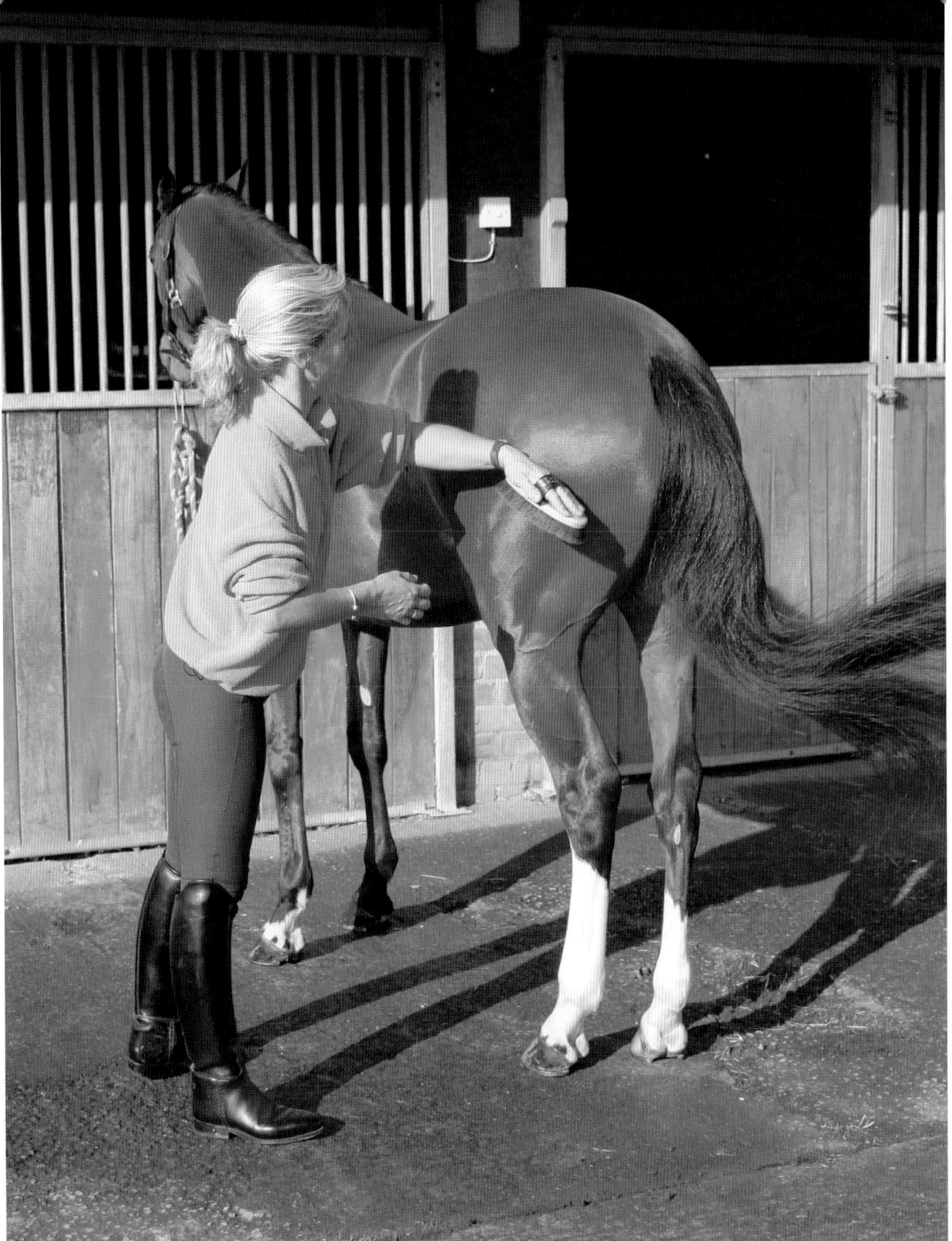

the roots of the mane and tail for cleanliness, and groom them gently, a process many horses enjoy.

For more information on wisping see page 151, in particular *Bodywork For Horses* and *100 Ways To Improve Your Horse's Health.*

Making a wisp

To make a wisp, twist a rope of hay about your own height, holding the end under your foot as you twist and pulling slightly to tighten it, adding more hay as you go. Keeping one end under your foot, form two loops in the other end slightly longer than your hand, turn them downwards, and pass them alternately and fairly tightly under the rest of the rope until you reach your foot. Tuck the remaining end under the top twist to secure it. Jump on it to harden and flatten it, and damp it slightly before use. It should last you about three or four uses.

65 Provide relief from physical irritation

Horses' reaction to physical irritation is to bite and kick themselves, or to find something convenient to rub on to get rid of the itch. Sometimes horses will present an itchy area to a friend who, being a horse, understands completely and obliges by scrubbing at the spot with his teeth. You can be just as valued a friend by relieving and treating your horse's irritations, and preventing them where possible.

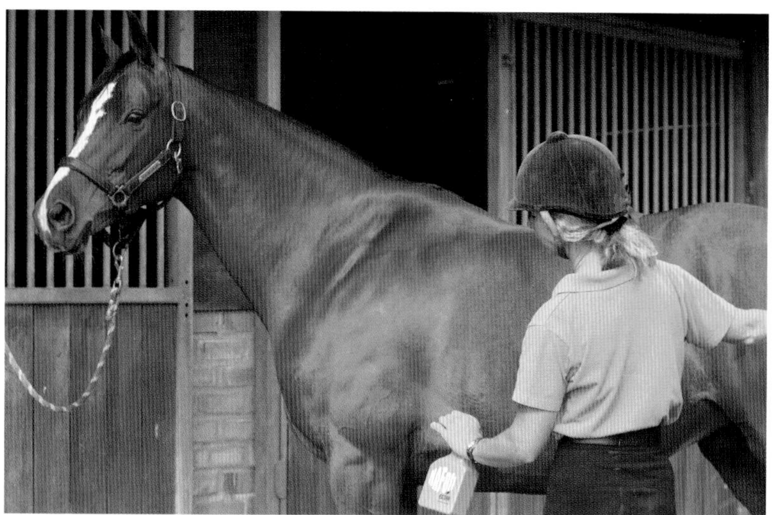

Insects

Thankfully a vaccine is being developed against sweet itch, and this could be the answer for many horses, ponies and their owners. Midge-proof mesh coveralls are very effective, though some tear easily. Fly repellents vary, but it is worth trying different brands, not only those for applying to the horse but the feed-additive types, too.

General fly relief for the head can be provided by means of bonnets and fringes (use the heavy, swinging cotton type) attached to a field-safe headcollar or halter. Although airy, shady field shelters (kept clear of droppings inside, like your paddocks) are a welcome haven in the fly seasons, make sure your horse is not being kept out by others. It may be kinder to keep him in a cool stable during the day, and turn him out at night.

Check clothing

When putting on your horse's rugs, blankets or sheets, check properly that the side going next to the horse is completely free from anything that could irritate him and perhaps eventually cause a sore place. Bits of bedding or hay caught on the lining are the main culprits, and the horse could be driven to distraction by a piece of bedding, a twig or bits of dried grass. He cannot remove it himself and could, in turn, rub himself extremely sore in his frustration.

Numnahs and saddle pads

The weight of both saddle and rider pressing down on debris that is caught on the saddle's underside, which in turn presses into the horse's skin, can cause a really sore place and considerable mental distress. Also, make sure that numnahs and pads are smoothed out, as wrinkles and folded-up corners cause uneven pressure and discomfort. All parts of the horse that will be under tack must first be freed of dried mud and other foreign bodies.

Fitting rugs and sheets

Many styles of rug must be extremely uncomfortable for the horse, as they press down on the withers, pull on the chest, the points of the shoulders and the tops of the forelegs, restrict his action and rub the croup and hips.

Only use rugs that really fit your horse without pulling or rubbing. Even a correctly sized rug can be the wrong shape for your particular horse, giving him many hours of real discomfort and distress. Most people use far too many rugs these days, making the horse itchy and overheated, even sweating. Always use as few as possible, and choose soft, comfortable materials.

66 Relieve psychological distress

Although many horses appear tolerant and laid back, often they have just developed a stoic attitude to life because they have learned from experience that they have no choice. We forget that our horses are, in reality, not only our slaves but also prisoners. We are in total control of every aspect of their lives and should, therefore, make things as pleasant as possible.

What causes distress?

Physical discomfort certainly causes distress, so relieving it is humane horse care. *Preventing* it is what we should really aim at.

Horses with even slight injuries can quickly become run down with the stress of constant discomfort or pain, plus the need to use unaccustomed muscles to move in a way that will lessen the pain: therefore we need to treat problems quickly and effectively. Wounds and insect stings can become really uncomfortable if not cared for, so we need to treat these correctly and regularly until they have healed completely.

Injuries such as sprains can be very painful and may need fairly strong painkillers for a while – just enough to lessen the worst of the pain for humane reasons, whilst still leaving the horse with enough discomfort to remind him not to stress the injured part. I certainly do not agree with the view that no painkillers should be given in these cases.

Other things that cause psychological distress are:

- overwork or unsuitable work;
- lack of company, particularly a special friend;
- lack of regular clean food and water;
- a feeling of being used, rather than cared about;
- minimal bedding systems, which leave horses holding their urine because of the dislike of splashing themselves, and with nowhere comfortable to lie down and rest;
- rough, loud handling;
- unknowledgeable, unsympathetic and inappropriate work or training techniques;
- being forced to do things that upset or frighten them; although some treatments such as farriery and veterinary attention are often unavoidable, horses should be trained and accustomed to such occasions, and professional advice should be taken in difficult cases.

How can I tell if my horse is distressed?

- The horse will usually have a worried, tense or frightened look about his face and body, with tight facial skin, pricked ears, wide eyes and flared nostrils, or a dull, closed-off and sad attitude.
- He may start to perform stereotypies (stable vices) and other abnormal behaviour.
- He could start to become difficult to handle, and his work could deteriorate.
- Patchy sweating can indicate pain; cold sweats indicate shock or exhaustion.

It is crucial to get to know your horse really well and not simply tell yourself that everything is all right when you suspect or know that it isn't.

67 Practise environmental enrichment

We read enough these days to leave us in no doubt that a conventional stable can be a very poor way to keep a horse, other than for short periods. Apart from altering stables or other housing so that horses can touch, smell and possibly mutual groom each other, and making them better ventilated and more spacious, enriching the horses' environment by means of one of their favourite things – food – is really easy.

What exactly is 'environmental enrichment'?

It simply means creating an environment that is more enjoyable, accommodating and stimulating for the horse to be in. We all know about the advantages of ad lib hay or haylage, depending on the horse's dietary needs, but most people just give the horse net after net or tub after tub of the same forage (hay or haylage) – forage meaning the type of food horses would naturally seek out for themselves, such as grasses and other plants.

Hay or haylage is the staple diet of most horses. Cut from a modern, specially sown ley (land temporarily under grass), the range of grasses in it may be very restricted, extremely so if you have a specialist hay, such as ryegrass hay, timothy hay, racehorse hay (usually a mixture of those two), mixture hay or seed hay. Artificially sown meadow hay will have more varieties in it, but usually not more than six to ten at the most. However, a crop cut from a meadow that has been maintained for many years as natural meadowland will have many more species and is by far the better choice. (Ask your vet or feed firm about having samples of your staple forage analysed periodically so that you have some idea of its nutritional content as a foundation for the rest of your horse's diet.)

In the wild, equines are able to forage on at least 50, and often many more, species of grasses, herbs, legumes and other plants. They can sniff out and dig up roots and tubers, browse on leaves from shrubs and trees, lick and bite bark and interesting earth and eat seasonal fruits and seeds. All these provide them with a wide variety of glorious smells, delicious tastes and a wide range of natural nutrients. Just as importantly, the horses get totally absorbing enjoyment, relaxation, mental stimulation, gentle physical exercise and fascinating occupation. No wonder they like being turned out.

Although we can provide horses' nutrient requirements by means of scientifically formulated feeds, supplements, and additives such as roots, in a stable there is no way we can provide the sheer variety of plants they experience naturally. Good hay and haylage are very welcome, but life can be made much more enjoyable and fulfilling for horses if we provide several different types of hay, haylage, and other forages such as chopped grasses and other plants now readily available on the market. All these can, in total, be given in amounts that make up the horse's 24-hour ration so that he gets what he needs, what he wants as far as possible, and enjoys the variety and, most importantly, the free choice of eating what he wants, when he wants it.

How do I decide what to give him?

As a conscientious owner, you will have a good idea of the energy and protein levels your horse needs and of his health status – whether or not he is prone to weight gain or laminitis, is elderly, young and growing, resting, in hard work and so on. Ring the free helplines at the feed company whose feeds you use (or try more than one!), tell them what you are planning, and check what feeds they make of a forage nature with the nutritional content your horse needs.

Most firms have at least a couple of different bagged forages that may contain lucerne/alfalfa, maybe clover, other related leguminous plants, several grasses and feeding straws such as oat or barley. These are chopped short and sometimes treated with light syrups or other sweeteners for palatability. Several different products will, of course, provide your horse with several different smells and tastes, which is just what you, and he, want.

As well as your horse's normal hay/haylage supply, try buying in some of a different crop and introduce it gradually so he has more choice of long forage.

How exactly do I put this into practice?

Fix up in the stable several containers for the different feeds you can obtain, and make available to your horse some of each all round the clock, as when grazing. This enables the micro-organisms in his gut to maintain stable, healthy populations and so helps to ensure his digestive efficiency.

Horses fed this way happily wander from one container to another, eating a bit of A, a bit of B, a bit of C, going back to B, chomping some haylage, then a bit of A again and so on. This mimics as best you can in a conventional stable his grazing behaviour of wandering about, filling his intestines and occupying his mind. Don't forget the succulents, such as carrots, soaked sugar-beet pulp, apples and so on.

Remember that horses should eat and drink with their heads down – at least lower than their withers – so low corner mangers and fixed, floor-standing tubs are best.

I have used this method of environmental enrichment with several horses, and it works beautifully. Do give it a go with your horses.

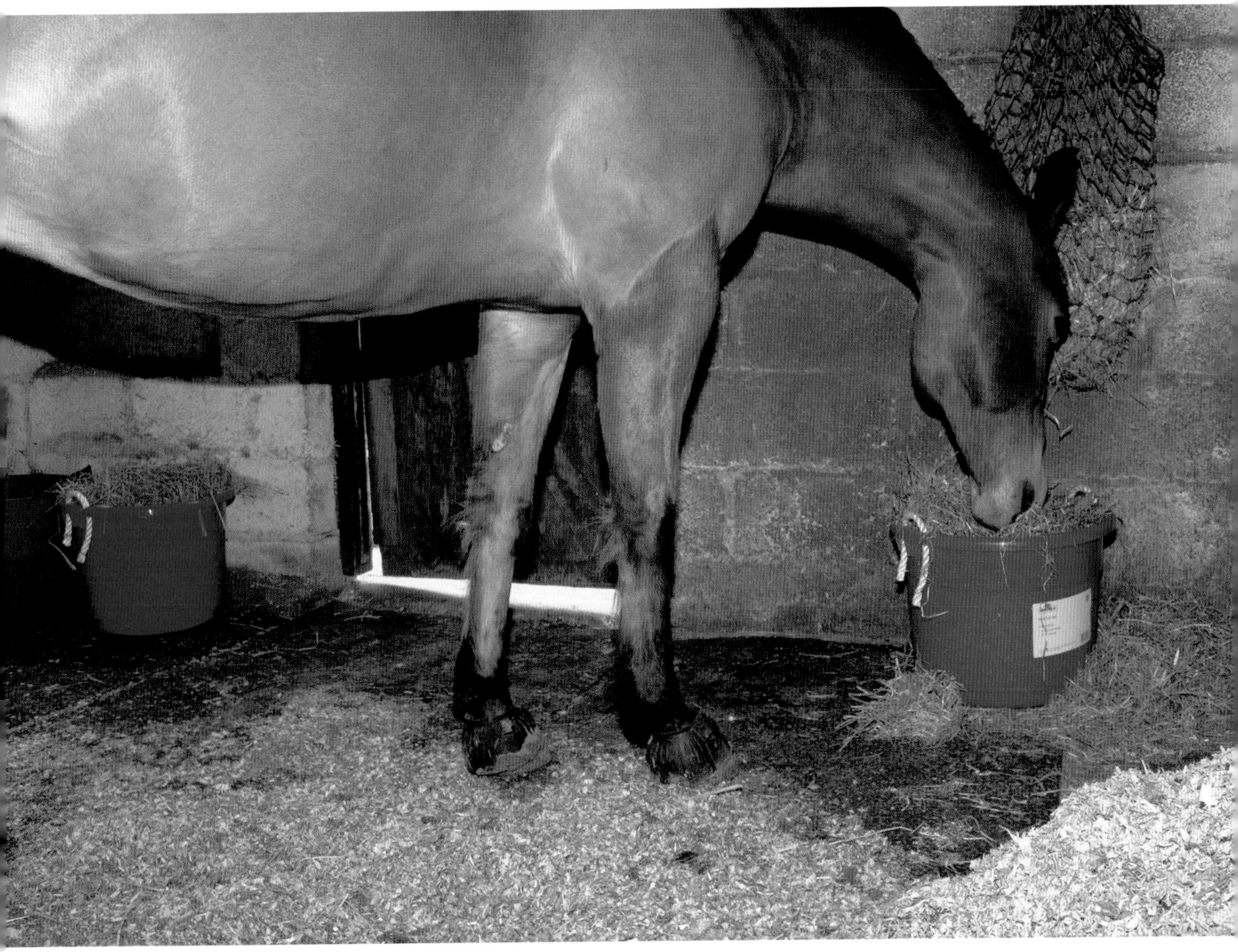

68 Protect your horse from bullies

A major problem on a communal yard such as a livery establishment is horse-to-horse relationships (human-to-human ones are sometimes even worse!). The stable bully's owner is paying her bills, too, and has just as much right as everyone else to turn her horse out. The legal situation, at least in the UK, regarding animals that injure others is confused: so let's look at the practicalities and some realistic solutions.

Not you again!

We're all familiar with bully behaviour – the bossy horse goes out looking for trouble, harassing other horses, pushing them about, splitting groups and sometimes not just being threatening, but actually biting, kicking and causing injuries.

Other horses have varying views of bullies. Self-confident, superior horses can easily see them off and occasionally protect others, but many horses of lower self-esteem or rank end up being chivvied from one point to another, unable to settle to grazing, constantly watching the bully's whereabouts and having to run away when he approaches. If this continues, such horses not only lose condition but soon learn to equate turnout with a frightening situation. In the longer term, being forced into the company of the bully can cause prolonged stress, which always adversely affects a horse's well-being.

It has also been suggested that if a horse's owner puts him out with another horse he is frightened of, this can at least partly destroy the horse's trust in his owner. The horse can also become difficult to lead towards or near the paddock, and one of the greatest pleasures of his life – grazing with friends – is denied him.

What can I do?

The obvious answer is to remove the bully. On your own premises this may be easy, but if you are a livery client, you and other affected owners must ask the yard proprietor to graze the bully elsewhere – and do not accept their playing down the problem, as some will.

In most yards there will be alternative grazing, and although paddocks need grazing, treating and resting in turn, a good yard will divide up grazing sufficiently to make it possible for all horses to graze safely with friends, not enemies. If not, it may be necessary to graze horses on a rota so that the bully is not out at the same time as horses he habitually harasses. Putting him into another herd of higher-ranking horses is one solution. As a last resort, you may need to find another yard or at least rent grazing elsewhere, only using your livery yard for stabling and other facilities – probably a rather inconvenient course of action.

69 Mutual groom with your horse

This recommendation may horrify traditionalists, who feel that any 'horsey' approach indicates a lack of manners towards, and respect for, humans. There are 'approaches' and 'approaches', however, and if you want a mutually respecting, affectionate relationship with your horse and not a master-servant one, spurning friendly advances won't enhance any good feelings your horse may have towards you.

What kinds of advances *aren't* friendly?

Clearly, any gestures that involve threatening faces, or attitudes such as ears back with muzzle out, nostrils wrinkled up and eyes aggressive, are anything but friendly. The same goes for horses who have a similar facial expression and turn their hindquarters to you, maybe with swishing tail and a hovering hind foot – both of these constituting a clear indication of their intention to kick.

Allowing some horses to rub their heads on you after removing their bridle may indicate that they regard you as inferior – although they should appreciate your scratching their itchy places with your hands. This is a service to them, although it apparently puts you in the senior position because you are doing it at your volition, not theirs. It depends on the horse's attitude towards you.

What does mutual grooming mean?

It is a term used to describe two horses standing head to tail rubbing each other's lower neck, withers and back with their muzzles and teeth. Rubbing this area firmly, as horses do, is known to lower their heart rate and help them relax; friends do it to each other as a token of friendship and to cement their bond.

It is clearly, then, a sign of acceptance and liking if your horse wants to mutual groom with you. You can see if your horse would like this by standing with your back to his head within reach and rubbing the area mentioned firmly with your fingertips. He may well start rubbing your back with his muzzle or teeth.

If he offers to do this to you when you are standing in the right position, take it as a compliment.

I used to teach at a livery yard where there was a sweet-natured horse who would mutual groom with anyone who let him. He also used to hug people with his head and neck. But his owner never permitted these things, and treated him purely as a means of winning prizes. Although everyone at the yard liked him and he had good horsey friends, he always had a sad air about him and I felt so sorry for him.

70 Work out a feel-good diet

Horse or human, we are all what we eat and drink. When you think about it, we can't be anything else, because what we take into our body is what it uses to construct and maintain itself, with the necessary input of the gases in the air we breathe. Inseparable from our body is our mind, that intangible entity that we often confuse with our brain: it has a profound effect on us, but is itself deeply affected by our diet.

Where do I start?

I am sure that most people do not realize the powerful effect that diet has on our body and mind. It therefore makes sense not only to take good advice, but also to learn as much as you reasonably can yourself so that you can judge, question and understand the more advanced literature. It's a good plan to learn in a structured way, rather than randomly, and a good place to start is with an understandable, science-based book (*The Horse Nutrition Bible* – see page 151).

Nutrition is a complex subject, but everyone can acquire a good working knowledge of it, and can then refine the details by consulting nutritionists. Most companies have websites and produce newsletters and literature on their products, and on feeding in general. Magazines publish articles on nutrition, and there are several excellent science-based books on the subject, plus distance-learning courses, DVDs – and, of course, the Internet.

I am very much in favour of the helplines now run by feed companies, whose qualified staff give excellent general feeding advice, not always pushing their own products.

On eating like a horse

We all know by now that horses evolved to eat mainly grass, with some other vegetation thrown in. Early horse types browsed leaves from trees and shrubs because grass had not evolved; most horses now eat both types of food if they have access to them.

Horses are adapted to thrive on poor quality, fibrous grasses of poor to moderate nutritional content compared with modern, improved grasses. Also, they are not adapted to thrive on a lot of starchy cereal grains such as oats, maize (corn) and barley – again, at least not the modern grains bred from earlier types.

Grasses and other fibrous plants are found in hay, haylage and commercial short-chopped forage feeds. Cereal grains are found in most coarse mixes (sweet feeds in the USA) and cubes or pellets, also called nuts. Good feed manufacturers produce different feeds with different ingredients for different categories of horse or pony, and their nutritionists will advise anyone enquiring about them as to the most suitable feed for their animal.

What can go wrong?

Modern, improved grasses are much less fibrous and contain more sugar than more primitive types. Horses have a sweet tooth, and when grazing will always seek out the sweetest, juiciest grasses. But if rich, sweet grass is eaten to excess it can cause serious long-term problems, such as obesity, colic, laminitis and uneven growth rates and inflamed joints in youngstock.

Too much starchy food has similar effects. If there is more starch than can be digested in the first part of the digestive tract – the foregut or small intestine – it gets pushed along, before it has been adequately broken down, into the large intestine or hindgut, where it cannot be dealt with effectively. This causes the formation of toxins, which can cause colic and other problems, excessive energy and erratic behaviour.

Obesity is as bad for horses as it is for us: no one feels comfortable when they are overweight – everything is an effort, and our bodies are under excess strain because of the extra weight we are carrying. Colic is extremely painful and frightening for horses: it simply means abdominal pain, which may not be linked to digestion. However, severe indigestion is called colic and can be triggered by too much and unsuitable food. Laminitis is also excruciatingly painful, and both colic and laminitis can result in the death or euthanasia of the horse or pony.

Underfed horses also do not feel good. Debility, being underweight, and even slight levels of malnutrition create weakness, depression or negativity, loss of confidence, lack of energy and a general failure to thrive.

What can I do?

To work out an appropriate diet for your horse, you could start by observing the following tenets:

- Always offer horses grass on the poorer side, and limit grazing for horses prone to putting on weight or already too fat, and those prone to laminitis.
- Base your stabled horse's diet on forage feeds (fibre such as hay, haylage and short-chopped forages, often incorrectly called 'chaff', which is actually the outside husk of grains).
- Only feed concentrates if your horse is genuinely not doing well enough on forage alone.
- Learn to condition score your horse. This means assessing his weight, probably every week, according to an established scale (see page 151; details are given in *100 Ways To Improve Your Horse's Health*).
- Learn to work out for yourself the appropriate energy level of your horse's diet and the correct amount to give him daily. You must be honest about his level of work so that you neither overfeed nor underfeed him. (Again, details are given in *100 Ways To Improve Your Horse's Health.*)
- Make good use of the helpline at the company whose feeds you use. Many people use feeds from different companies, but qualified nutritionists are unlikely to give you conflicting information. A vet interested in nutrition is also a great help.

71 Sponge down your horse thoughtfully

Bathing horses seems to be one of the favourite pastimes of many horse owners, although it was rarely seen years ago. The way it is done makes a big difference to how horses view it: some really enjoy it, but others hate it and are truly terrified of it. It is not a necessary procedure but provided it is done with pre-planning, with consideration for the horse as a flesh and blood creature, and with a caring attitude, it can be helpful.

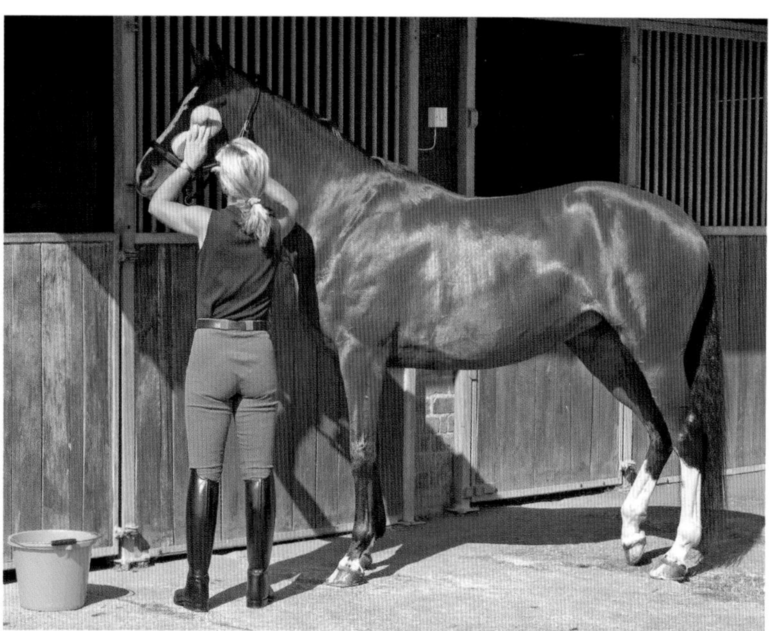

The most important Golden Rule: do not use cold water!

Dousing with cold water is a standard torture technique in human society. What many owners of horses and other animals overlook, or do not care about because they aren't on the receiving end of it, is that they are warm-blooded animals just like us – and *very* few people genuinely enjoy bathing or showering or swimming in cold water. Some say they do, just to appear tough and to attract attention to themselves, but the truth is usually very different.

Cold water is a tremendous shock to the system, which is not good for any mammalian body. Humans (unless being tortured) may have some choice in the matter, but horses usually do not; even if they make their feelings known, they are normally restrained and coerced into accepting it – 'training', some call it. Surely most right-minded people would admit that all this amounts to cruelty.

If you have your own yard, fit a basic water heater in the stable area so you always have access to hot water. If not, take plenty of very hot water to your livery yard in camping-sized vacuum containers to add to the cold water.

Consider whether spongeing down is really necessary

Horses who are regularly and properly groomed should not need washing down. Those who are very greasy and dirty may need it, but it is not the best way to maintain a horse's coat. Using shampoo or soap can wash out too much of the natural oil in the skin and coat, removing their protection and the hair's natural gloss.

Assess the weather

Look at, and feel, the weather carefully. Few yards have a protected washing area, so if you have to do your horse outdoors he will feel the cold intensely and quickly on a chilly day. Consider instead hot-towelling him (see page 151, particularly *The Horse Owner's Essential Survival Guide* and *Bodywork For Horses*).

Water temperature

Whether bathing or spongeing down after hard work, use lukewarm or tepid water on a hot day, as this will cool and refresh your horse. On a fairly cool day, use water that feels warm to hand-hot to your bare hand.

72 Create varied grazing

Modern 'green desert' pastures are going out of fashion as landowners and stud managers realize the advantages of providing a wide variety of grasses and other plants for their horses. Even so, most of the pastures available to most horses are restricted in their range of vegetation and are too rich in nutritional content, being leftovers from farming land once used for dairy and beef cattle.

What's wrong with farmland?

There is nothing wrong with farmland, as long as it is used for cattle. Cattle are more efficient digesters of grass than horses, and dairy cattle in particular need highly nutritious grass, for lactation is extremely demanding on an animal's body and system.

When such land is used for horses, even Thoroughbred breeding stock, the problems mentioned on pages 106–107 can arise. Conversely, when cattle (usually beef cattle) or sheep are used to 'top' horse paddocks (eat off the grasses the horses have declined), they can use the fibrous remains more effectively than horses and, unlike them, are not put off by the smell of horse droppings that will probably be contaminating the paddock, even when these are picked up on a daily basis.

What is the best pasture for horses?

Horses need grass of moderately high nutrient (sugar/protein) content if breeding or working fairly hard. Horses, and especially ponies, in only light work or resting need low nutrient grasses similar to the pasture used in sheep farming. Seed merchants and land advisers now produce, or can obtain, seed mixes for any category of equine, from resting Shetland ponies to Thoroughbred bloodstock and high performance horses.

What are the best grasses, in general, for horses?

A general, multi-purpose sward for a variety of horses, not too rich and not too poor, might contain the following grasses that are palatable to horses:

- Smooth- and rough-stalked meadow grasses
- Red fescue
- Meadow fescue
- Timothy
- Ryegrass (any)
- White clover (rather than red): this should comprise no more than 10 per cent of the pasture.

For ponies or resting cobs or warmbloods and similar types, some grasses that are not so highly 'palatable' should be included, perhaps in quite high proportions, such as sheep's fescue, cocksfoot and bent. Yorkshire fog is regarded as a poor grass for horses, and many will not touch it.

Take the advice of your adviser, who may be from a commercial firm or an employee of DEFRA in the UK (your local County Extension Agent in the USA). State clearly that your pasture is for horses of a stipulated category, and ask for as wide a variety as possible of suitable grasses and other plants.

Include a separate herb strip on the sunniest and driest part of your land. Herbs sown with grass tend to be smothered by actively growing grasses.

73 Feed enough fibre

'Fibre', 'forage', 'roughage' and 'bulk' are words usually used to represent feeds such as hay, haylage, feeding straws and grass. The horse's natural food is grass, and the others are conserved, dried forms of grass. Cereal crops from which straw comes are domestically developed versions of grasses. For horses, eating grass gives maximum pleasure, an experience followed very closely by that of eating other forms of fibre.

Why is fibre so important to horses?

Fibre is an essential food for horses because it is what they can best digest and thrive on. It is a fairly complete and physically satisfying source of nutrients for horses doing little to moderate work and sometimes quite hard work; much depends on the type of horse or pony and the quality and nutrient content of the fibre. Just as importantly, it satisfies their evolutionary psychological needs by providing them with almost endless mental occupation. Horses are by nature not well equipped to be either bored or hungry.

A bit of science

Horses' intestines hold a *lot* of food, and most of this is meant to be fibre. Fibre is a 'structural carbohydrate'. Carbohydrates are compounds (foods made up of more than one ingredient) containing carbon, hydrogen and oxygen and comprising cellulose, sugars and starch. They are sub-divided into non-structural carbohydrates (sugars and starches) and structural carbohydrates (fibre). Fibre is the type of carbohydrate, therefore, that is found in the cell walls of plants and which gives them their structure and strength.

The fibrous part of the diet is composed of:

- **Lignin**: woody, indigestible and non-nutritious fibre that bulks out the intestines, stimulates peristalsis (the wave-like movements of the intestines that move the food along) and physically breaks up the food.
- **Cellulose**: structural carbohydrate that is digested by being fermented by micro-organisms in the hind gut or large intestine, producing low levels of 'slow-release' energy over several hours.
- **Hemi (half) cellulose**: structural carbohydrate that is easier to digest than cellulose, and gives more energy.

Most foods, whether hay, haylage, grass, other plants or cereals, contain some of each of carbohydrate, protein and fats (oils, also called lipids and lipins), and also water. The advantages of fibre are as follows:

- It is the horse's natural food and must comprise the major portion of his diet for health and digestive comfort.
- It helps to store water and electrolytes in the hind gut, thereby helping to prevent dehydration.
- It continues to provide slow-release energy for body functioning, warmth and work for up to several hours after its ingestion.
- The type of energy it produces does not create the problems associated with sugar or starch unless it is eaten to excess; this applies mainly to nutritionally enhanced domestic grass species.
- It is essential for the efficient and healthy working of the digestive tract.
- Seeking and selecting different forages provides the horse with many hours of relaxing, reassuring, interesting and satisfying occupation – a highly important factor in maintaining a horse who is healthy in body and mind, and content in his home life.

Time budgets

Studies on horses show that outdoor horses on reasonable pasture spend about 16 to 18 hours out of 24 grazing and browsing, yarded horses spend slightly less, and stabled horses spend considerably less, even when provided with ad lib forage. The horse's natural time expenditure, therefore, comprises approximately 17 hours eating and about four or five hours sleeping, leaving only two to four hours for other things such as drinking, socializing, standing resting and dozing, and body maintenance such as rolling and rubbing.

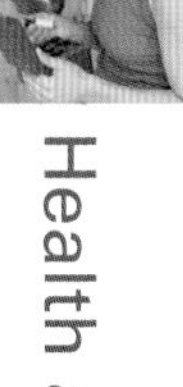

The problem with grass

The type of pasture most domestic horses are turned out on is very different from natural grazing. Often it is too nutritious, causing problems of the horse becoming overweight, which can easily lead to actual obesity. Grass also stores non-structural carbohydrates called fructans as a future energy source, and these are currently believed to trigger laminitis. Therefore, eating too much grass of too high a nutrient content is bad for horses. Most horses thrive on grass of low nutrient content, ideally growing over as large an area as possible so they have to move around a lot in order to find enough.

How much is enough?

Horses doing moderate to no work can probably do well on an all-fibre diet, with the possible addition of a broad-spectrum vitamin and mineral supplement or a feed balancer. These make up nutrients that may be lacking in their normal diet. Ask the nutritionist at the company whose feeds you use, which would be best for your horse.

Horses doing moderate to hard work may need higher energy fibre such as forage feeds based on lucerne/alfalfa, maybe with the addition of soaked sugar-beet pulp and/or oil for added energy. Some such horses may need a few cereals added. For horses in this category, probably not less than three-quarters of their diet by weight should be fibre/forage.

Horses doing hard, strenuous work may need more cereals adding to their diet, but the general advice today is that fibre should comprise not less than two-thirds by weight of the horse's diet, otherwise his digestive efficiency and comfort can be adversely affected.

See page 151 for more details on appropriate feeding, particularly *100 Ways To Improve Your Horse's Health*.

74 Don't feed concentrates unless necessary

Concentrates, more usually called cereals now, are little bundles of concentrated, high-energy starch and sugar wrapped up in inner and outer husks made of fibre – grains. They are called concentrates because, weight for weight, they contain much more energy than fibre. However, the type of energy they contain is not always good for some horses, such as medium-weight and heavyweight animals, and especially not for cobs and ponies.

Why are concentrates not always suitable for horses?

The horse's digestive tract has changed very little since horses were first domesticated around 6,000 years ago. It still operates best on a mainly fibrous diet (see previous pages), but many horses in hard or strenuous work, which is more physically demanding on them than anything they would do naturally, do need an energy boost to help them, and this is given to them in the form of cereal grains.

The main cereals fed to horses in Westernized countries are oats, maize (corn) and barley, with some wheat products to a lesser extent. The starchy energy these provide is more readily available to the horse than the energy from cellulose (fibre), which takes longer to digest but is available over a much longer period. Starch and sugar are digested in the small intestine or foregut by enzymes (instead of in the large intestine or hind gut by micro-organisms), and can be absorbed into the bloodstream comparatively quickly as glucose.

If the glucose is not going to be used immediately for energy to create heat, or for use as fuel for work, the body converts it to glycogen and stores it in the muscles and liver until it is needed. Some may be converted to fat and stored in various depots around the body.

The main problems arise when higher levels of cereals are fed than the animal needs and than his digestion can cope with. Horses usually love cereals, so they will eat them happily in large amounts – except in the case of, for example, some racing Thoroughbreds, who can become what horsemen used to call 'corn sick' (simply, sick of cereals and off their feed, partly because not enough fibre was being fed). Warmbloods, cold-blooded horses and native types do well on much less energy than hot-blooded horses, which is why cereals are often surplus to their needs.

If too much starchy food is given, the digestive tract does not have time to digest all of it before it is moved on by the movements of the intestine. This results in undigested starch being passed into the large intestine, which does not have the enzymes to process it. The micro-organisms here cannot really deal with it either, so the starch starts to ferment, producing toxic lactic acid as the end product of this process. The horse gets indigestion, basically, and the chemical balance of the large intestine is disrupted. This changed chemical environment in the gut kills off or seriously disables the micro-organisms that digest the fibrous part of the horse's diet, so you also get undigested fibre and therefore problems on both counts.

Some of these toxins can be absorbed back into the bloodstream, and will then damage or over-stress body tissues and organs, such as the kidneys (the blood filters of the body) and the liver (the body's 'food factory', one of whose many jobs is to transform poisons into simpler or more complex substances to protect the body from their adverse effects).

Moderately excessive amounts of cereals may simply result in excess weight, but larger amounts can result in colic and maybe also azoturia or 'tying up', now more commonly called ERS (equine rhabdomyolysis syndrome) and laminitis.

Concentrate feeds

Cereal concentrates are sold as straights (a single type of grain), cubes/nuts/pellets or coarse mixes/sweet feeds. With reputable brands there is always an analysis panel, strip or label on the bag so that you have a good idea of the nutritional content of the product. If you cannot understand it, do not hesitate to ask your supplier or to ring the manufacturer directly.

A vital piece of information that is usually missing is the level of energy in the feed. This is because the tests that need to be done on horses to determine a fairly precise energy level are so invasive that they would result in the destruction of the horse and so are not carried out for humane reasons. However, you can ask for this important information as well, and the description of the product will give you a good idea – racehorse nuts, pony cubes, low-energy mix and so on.

Look also for the declaration of ingredients. The item present in the highest proportion is given first, the second next and so on, so you know whether the feed you are considering is mainly fibre with a sprinkling of cereals, or nearly all cereals, or whatever. The product literature will also give you an idea of what your horse might need, but again it is best to be as certain as possible by asking the manufacturer, whose representative (a nutritionist) will ask exactly the type, height and constitution of your horse, plus his work level. You should be really accurate about this, for your horse's sake.

The upside of cereals

Apart from giving an energy boost when needed, glucose from cereals is the main source of energy needed by the brain and other organs, so if your horse or pony can take them, some may be helpful.

Sugar is also provided by soaked sugar-beet pulp, of course, and young, growing grass, being at its highest levels during daylight and at its lowest at night.

75 Create a 'help list'

Even if you are fortunate enough to be able to keep your horses at home, there will probably be times when you need someone to help you, perhaps when you are ill, working overtime, away for a day or more, and so on. Any kind of animal can be a tie, depending on your outlook, but it is quite possible to live a fairly free life if you have the right kind of help with your horses.

Qualities needed in helpers

There are several personal qualities needed in people you might ask to help you with your horses occasionally, whether you pay them or not:

They must know enough about horses to do the tasks properley. If these are just filling hay tubs or nets, removing droppings from the stable whilst the horses are out, filling water buckets and so on, then horse knowledge is not needed – though to be on the safe side they do need to know horses well enough to be able to check them and recognize good health from sickness and injury. And if you want the horses brought in or turned out, rugs seen to, or slightly difficult horses handled wisely, you need someone more knowledgeable and confident – especially if you want them to exercise and groom.

They must be reliable so that you know they are going to turn up – it is surprising how many people think nothing of breaking promises and arrangements. If they really cannot come for any reason, they must, at the very least, let you know.

They must be trustworthy so you know they will do, fully and properly, exactly what you have asked them to do, that they will not abuse your horses, damage your property, steal your belongings, or leave the place unsecured each time they leave.

They must be responsible so that if the unusual occurs, they will use their own initiative to cope with it. If they find your horse down with colic and can't get in touch with you, they must take the responsibility of calling the vet, preferably your own, but any vet, rather than delaying the matter until you can be reached. They must be responsible enough to attend to minor mishaps themselves, such as removing a badly damaged rug which could cause an accident, bodging up a broken fence rail or getting it mended to keep horses in during your absence, attending to a minor injury, and so on.

Try to have the names and reliable contact details of several suitable people, be they friends and family, agency staff or freelancers, so you are always covered. You may pay them (in money) or help them in some way in return. This could prove to be a beneficial arrangement for both of you.

From your horse's point of view, he will feel secure knowing that someone will always be there soon to see to his needs.

76 Clip and trim sparingly

Many people nowadays seem to clip and trim just because 'everyone else' does so, and very often horses and ponies are clipped and trimmed to the point of discomfort. But clipping and overtrimming a horse merely to 'smarten him up' is not a good enough reason to deprive him of his natural protection. How far you need to go depends on your horse, his job and his management.

Types of clip

The various types of clip with which we are familiar were devised to cater for different kinds of horse doing different jobs. It is best to clip only just enough to enable a horse to do his job comfortably, whilst leaving him enough coat to keep him comfortable when he is not working.

When they are not working horses are always more comfortable with their natural coats, unencumbered by clothing which is often really uncomfortable. Your horse will feel much happier, therefore, if he does not associate you with feeling uncomfortable, cold, too hot, weighed down by too many and too heavy rugs, or having to put up with the long-lasting and often severe discomfort of rugs that pull, press on the withers, rub and simply do not fit.

How can I decide which clip is suitable for my horse?

Here are some suggestions:

- If your horse is doing little or no work, do not clip him.
- If he is in light to moderate work at weekends but hardly working during the week, consider an Irish or trace clip and a judicious trim: under the jaw, the hair that grows outside the edges of the ears especially at their base, the mane trimmed to a flattering length, fetlocks trimmed with scissors and comb, and perhaps the tail banged halfway down his cannons, but not pulled at the top – all of this depending on breed, of course.
- For horses in moderate work and with very thick, naturally greasy coats, a 'chaser clip will make them easier to clean and will minimize sweating.
- A blanket clip is good for hard-working horses who work outdoors, as it leaves crucial protection over the back, loins and hindquarter muscle-mass areas, which need to be warm to work properly.

I do not believe that hunter and full clips are ever necessary for the horse's well-being. If any clip could be less suitably named it is the hunter clip, because the sides, loins and hindquarters are exposed, which is *not* good for horses who get hot following hounds and then have to stand around during checks and draws. A full clip removes all the coat, and is truly unkind to the horse, in my view, especially one working outdoors.

77 Introduce clippers considerately

Horses put up with a great deal from us, often without complaining. Clipping is one of those jobs a lot of horses do complain about, usually because they are not carefully introduced to it. In most cases it is the noise, but blunt, hot blades or a careless person doing the clipping can cause nicks, pulls, pain and fear. It is vital to take both care and time on every occasion that you clip, but especially the first few times.

Types of clipper

Most people still use electrically operated clippers that plug into a power source. These are fine, of course, but you have to be careful of the flex. Piling it in a plastic bucket is a good way to keep it under control. There are battery-operated clippers which remove this problem, cool-run clippers, quiet clippers and, of course, hand-operated barbers' clippers. The ideal, if you can find them, are battery-operated, cool-run, quiet clippers.

Introducing the clippers

If you have an electric grooming machine, your horse will take to clippers much more readily because of the noise of the motor and the slight pull on his skin from the brushes.

It is a good plan to introduce clippers before you actually clip. Let the horse see other horses being done, if possible. It is scientifically proven that if you feed titbits to a horse whilst he is experiencing something unpleasant, he concentrates more on the goodies and associates the task with them in the future.

Switch on the motor out in the yard and let it run for a few minutes whilst you groom the horse, and watch his reaction. Behave quietly and normally; don't coo and calm him down if he is merely showing curiosity. If he appears frightened, don't approach any closer and don't say 'good boy', as this is praising him for being alarmed. Say 'easy' or something low and drawn out, and generally he will soon stop making too much of a fuss.

Have the clippers in one hand and stroke his shoulder firmly with your other hand. Next, rest the clipper on top of your hand so that he can feel the vibrations through it, stroking him this way. Then rest the body of the clipper on his shoulder next to your hand, and move the two further along his body towards the tail, thus allowing him to get used to feeling it in various places. It's up to you at which point on his body you start clipping – and you do this as a smooth continuation of the 'feeling' process – but it's normally best to begin around the middle of the horse, away from the head but not too near the back end.

If you are not an accomplished clipper, engage a professional for your horse's first few clips, but be sure to be there with him.

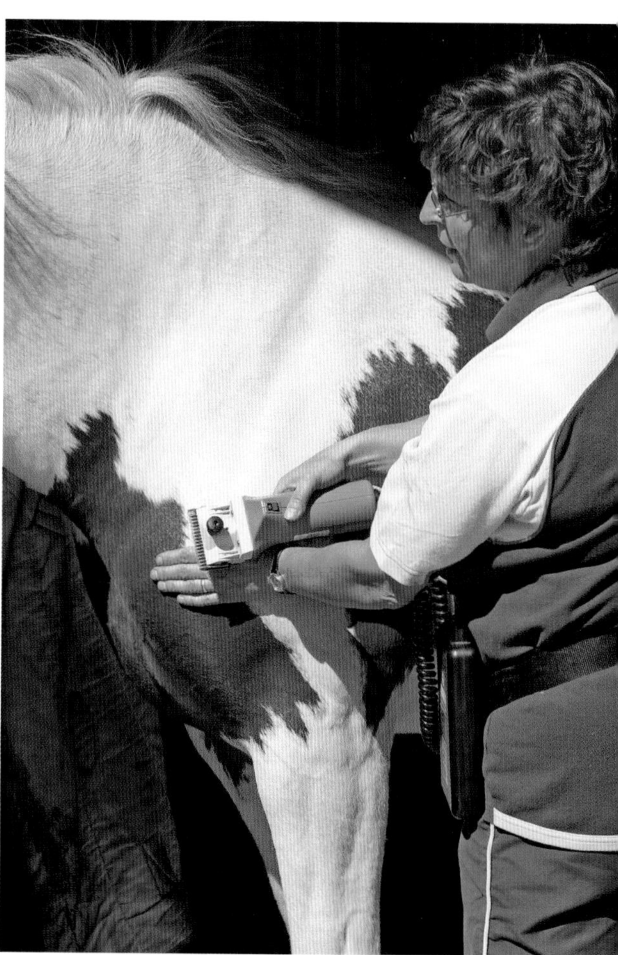

78 Never remove your horse's 'whiskers'

It amazes me that people who say they love their horses continue to remove their whiskers around the eyes and muzzle, as if there were some unwritten law that compelled them to do so. Presumably these people would never do this to their rabbit, cat or dog, but they inflict it on their horses without a thought. Some breed societies and other showing organizations are now regulating against it, and I wish they all would. I understand that the practice has actually been made illegal in Germany.

The horse's sense of touch

The correct name for these feeler whiskers is 'vibrissae'. They are found around the eyes and muzzle, partly as protectors and partly as information-gatherers. They help to prevent the horse banging his head by informing him how far away he is from objects, walls and so on, and help him to investigate things such as electric fencing ('is it on or off?') or new things in his environment without actually having to touch them with his skin.

When horses touch things, sensory or afferent nerves in the skin send messages to the brain, giving information about the type of sensation distinguished. The vibrissae are clearly quite different from all other hairs on the body and have a generous supply of afferent nerves, so are without doubt a significant part of the sense of touch and should certainly not be removed. To do so is at the least thoughtless and callous, I feel.

Other mammals with vibrissae are known to use them to help them, for instance, pass through openings, feel things in the dark, and as a warning system to protect the head, which contains all the other senses.

Results of removing vibrissae

Many people notice that horses may be prone to knocking their heads more after the vibrissae have been clipped off, and that some horses actually go off their feed because they use these hairs to help them feel what they are eating. When travelling, horses are, of course, in a more precarious situation as far as their balance is concerned, and those who have recently had their whiskers removed do seem to bang their heads more, and may even be unable to balance quite as well as others. Although the hairs are not part of the balancing mechanism, the horses clearly feel compromised without them. And all this is quite unnecessary and unkind.

People remove the whiskers for the dubious reason of 'smartness' and 'tidiness', and seem quite smug about it, as if they enjoy doing it. In my view, horses without their whiskers simply look deprived, which they are. Because some organizations are now regulating against their removal, perhaps it could be said, as has been suggested to me in conversation, that those that don't, do not have the interests of the horses at heart...

79 Pander to your horse's likes and dislikes

The title of this topic might give the wrong idea to some readers, and I would say at the outset that it does not mean giving your horse all his own way (and some will say 'what's wrong with that?) or allowing him to become a wayward, unruly hoodlum if he is that way inclined. It means giving him a life that is interesting, enjoyable, pleasurable, comfortable, secure and content – which is what we all want.

From angel to devil

Some horses are easy to look after and work with. They seem to go along with whatever you present to them (within reason), they eat anything you offer them, seem happy to come in and go out whenever you wish, will work anywhere, hack anywhere, at least try to do whatever you ask, and generally seem to want to be your other half.

Some are just as predictable the other way: they always seem to be in a bad mood, ready to kick and bite gratuitously. They maintain a personal vendetta against every rider, protect their territory with a vengeance, and are hair-raising to ride.

Others are, shall we say, challenging. You never know what mood they are going to be in, and range from angel to devil. You may often have to cajole them to do anything, they look with dislike at a bucket of feed you have carefully sourced and made up, and stand and weave or head-toss if you don't bring something more acceptable. On some days, for no apparent reason, they don't want to be turned out, and on others they don't want to come in. They may happily go where you want and do what you ask, or they may refuse point blank to do anything. On the days when they greet you with threatening hindquarters and a swishing tail you really wonder why you bother, but it suddenly all seems worthwhile when they come up to you and put their head in your arms for a cuddle.

How can I tell what he wants?

This often takes time, perception and feel, but sometimes you just click with a particular horse and get a good understanding of him almost instantly.

I have had horses, both my own and complete strangers, 'call' to me mentally with some need or request, sometimes when I wasn't looking at, or even thinking about them, but sometimes when I was. Anyone can cultivate this ability by being calm in mind and body, and by learning to switch to 'neutral' mentally. This seems to give the messages a chance to get through from the horse's mind to yours, like an open channel.

One of the best ways I know to get an idea of how a horse feels and what he wants, and to let the messages flow, even if you do not know him, is to approach him completely open-mindedly and stand quietly with him. Contrary to fashionable opinion, look him in the eye, but softly, and stand just out of reach until you can tell from the look on his face and the attitude of his head and neck whether or not he welcomes you, or you need to keep your distance for a while (in which case stay put for a time and you'll get something before long).

A basic knowledge of body language is needed for this (see page 151, particularly *100 Ways To Improve Your Horse's Behaviour* and *The Horse Behaviour Handbook*). Basically, ears back, a cross or aggressive look in the eye, nostrils wrinkled up and perhaps the muzzle extended towards you on a 'snaking' neck mean 'don't you dare come near me'. Ears pricked towards you or held softly, an 'open', soft eye, relaxed nostrils and relaxed head and neck posture mean that the horse will allow, or invite, you closer so that he can smell you.

Everyday experience

Looking after, handling and riding a horse regularly and trying different things with him will give any open-minded person plenty of information as to what he likes or dislikes. You could try different foods, different treats, also different hacking routes, school exercises, types of tack and clothing, and bodywork and grooming techniques, and then watch and feel his reactions.

But *why* should I pander to him?

You should pander to him simply because this will cause him to associate you with pleasure, comfort, safety, feeling good and everything else good. If you know he genuinely dislikes or fears something, don't put him 'through it' unless you really must, and not just because someone is haranguing you to 'make him have it'. Of course, sensitive professional help could well get your horse over these things and widen his horizons, to the benefit of both of you.

Horses are not so stupid that they cannot tell whether or not you care about them. They also know very well whether or not you can be manipulated or deserve co-operation. Ignore the prognostications of those who clearly have no real heart for horses, no matter how famous they are. Watch and 'feel' the horses of these people, then decide whether or not they seem truly content and fulfilled. It may come as a considerable shock to you to discover that often they are not.

80 Give enough, and regular, turnout

It's true that many horses, both famous ones and the unknown, are rarely or even never turned out. I have experienced a lot of these unfortunate characters throughout my life and can categorically state that horses allowed freedom frequently and regularly are happier, better balanced, more fulfilled, amenable and settled than those denied this basic right all or most of the time, no matter how well kept in other respects.

Excuses for not turning out

- With horses kept for a purpose rather than for themselves, a common excuse is that they are 'too valuable' to risk being injured by other horses or by their own antics.
- On some yards, the landowners seem to prefer the sight of empty, green, smooth-rolled fields to horses enjoying their birthright, and deny them their freedom.
- Where land is wet in winter, landowners will not want it poached and damaged, and so deny turnout on pasture; but they then fail to provide adequate surfaced areas for liberty.
- Horses who are hard to catch are often never turned out because their owners do not know how, or can't be bothered to retrain them.
- Keeping horses clean is another highly inexcusable pretext for not turning out.

Why turnout is so important

Freedom gives horses the chance to move freely and naturally at whatever gait they wish, provided the area is big enough, this is the way they would move all the time if they were living naturally. It also helps to maintain health and partial fitness, and gives the horses a much more interesting and stimulating environment.

Alternatives to grassland turnout

Although grass turnout is far preferable to anything else for any horse, there are times when it is not a good idea, such as when the ground is extremely wet, when horses would damage it, or when horses or ponies are prone to laminitis or would quickly become overweight, when very restricted grass consumption may be necessary.

In these cases, some other area should be created for them. I have been campaigning for years for more livery yards and equestrian businesses to create 'playpen' areas for horses, which would be better than no turnout at all. Most yards have spaces that are not fully used, which could be fenced off and used for a leg-stretch. These may be earth or could be surfaced with whatever is available locally, such as sand or bark chips.

Some people do not like horses being turned loose in their manège because of the risk of damaging or raising the membrane (a subject already addressed elsewhere in this book, see page 82; see also page 151 for an alternative construction method, described in *The Horse Owner's Essential Survival Guide*).

There is also a good case for creating a working area without a membrane where horses can be jumped and worked loose.

81 Be sure your horse likes his companions

Natural herd life enables horses to socialize with whatever other horses or ponies they wish. Herds are family groups, where long-term bonds build up that are rarely possible in domestic circumstances. Horses are also free to avoid those with whom they do not get on. But in a field or paddock, unless it is very large, this is not possible, and being kept in enforced proximity to animals whom they dislike or fear is very stressful.

How can I know whom he likes and whom he doesn't?

You can tell whom he likes by spending time watching his reactions to other horses, ideally when turned out with them, or at least when they are near each other on the yard, or are being ridden together or close to each other.

Signs of liking another horse are that the horses will graze very close to each other. Horses appear to have a personal oval around their bodies extending several feet away, into which only 'preferred associates' are allowed. Any horse that is allowed within this magic oval is surely liked, and good friends often graze actually touching each other, regularly mutual groom each other, and perform fly-removal services by standing head to tail and whisking away the flies from each other's faces.

Signs of dislike are keeping away, ears back, nostrils wrinkled up and back, threat signs such as muzzle extended and sometimes even teeth showing, or turning the hindquarters and threatening to kick, or actually doing so. Entire males and some geldings strike out with a front leg in warning, and so do a few strong-minded mares.

How does this affect our relationship?

As discussed on page 104, being forced to be near a disliked or feared animal causes prolonged stress. If your horse associates your turning him out with an unpleasant or frightening time or experience, he may lose trust in you, perhaps become difficult about being handled in these circumstances, and generally become upset. This is not the way to maintain a close partnership.

What can I do?

Do not force your horse to be in close contact with another horse or pony that he dislikes or fears in the field or any other turnout area, and do not stable them near each other, either. Arrange turnout for them at different times, and ideally in different fields, as they will still be able to smell each other. Ideally, they should be stabled out of both sight and earshot of each other, or as far apart as possible, certainly not nearby. This can cause difficulties on livery yards, but if the owner or manager will not help improve matters your horse will be living in a state of frequent distress or fear, or at least discontent, and you will be obliged to find other accommodation.

82 Learn 'home' bodywork techniques

If there is one thing most horses love, it is pleasurable attention from someone who clearly cares about them, and whom they like. It is perfectly natural for them to accept this attention, as it is like mutual grooming from another horse. Even though it is not the same technique, it has the same effect and works to bond horse and owner, relax and please both, and strengthen their partnership.

But don't I risk hurting my horse?

You certainly do not risk harming your horse in any way. The techniques I am thinking of are beneficial and completely safe, provided you are conscientious, read up on them and apply them sensibly. Any concerned therapist will book an appointment to show you some basic techniques to help your horse on a daily basis, if you wish. They all understand that most owners will call in a professional (see photographs) when needed, but cannot afford to do so very frequently. For a good working knowledge of suitable techniques for owners to perform on their own horses, see page 151, in particular *Bodywork for Horses* and *Complementary Therapies for Horse and Rider*. Meanwhile, let's see what's possible.

Body-brushing and grooming

We have already discussed grooming and wisping (strapping) as therapy on pages 98–99. These practices will probably come most easily to owners: you brush and groom your horse on most days, and it is simple to extend the process into as much of a therapy as a basic cleaning exercise.

Hand rubbing

This is another really simple technique that does a lot of good, calming and relaxing horses, stimulating the skin and underlying muscles, drying and cleaning and certainly creating a grounded, feel-good aura in the horse.

You use the flat of your bare hands and your bare forearms. The horse must be clean, as you don't want to rub dirt into his coat and skin, and he can be dry or damp. Let him eat hay or whatever fibre he normally has, as this will also relax him. The method is to use a little more pressure on muscled areas, but to go more gently on sensitive and bony areas. Stand with one foot slightly in front of the other, slightly stiffen your arms and lean your weight on and off on to your arms and hands; this is less tiring than pushing the horse, and more comfortable for him.

Massage

This is an extension of hand rubbing. Simple techniques sensibly applied are helpful in:

- keeping your horse's muscles healthy, pliable and able to work well;
- encouraging circulation, with all its benefits;
- loosening up and relieving muscles after working;
- assisting healing, and
- promoting the free flow of the body's energy or 'life force' by stimulating acupressure points and energy meridians or channels;
- encouraging the production of the body's natural painkillers and feel-good chemicals such as cortisol, endorphins and encephalins.

Do not massage directly on injured areas, but with advice, massage very gently around them to help diperse excess fluids and energy. Also, do not massage animals with a systemic disease (such as influenza, for instance), or pregnant mares.

Two simple techniques are *effleurage* and *clapping*:

Effleurage is relaxing and is simply stroking (like hand rubbing) but in a more structured way. Place your relaxed hands on your horse so they follow the shape of the tissues beneath them, slightly stiffen your arms with bent elbows, lean your weight on them and, working in the direction of the hair, move the skin over the underlying muscles with significant but comfortable pressure. You will get to know what your horse likes by his reaction. Work towards the heart. To do the legs, link your fingers and use your palms and the heels of your hands to work carefully upwards.

Clapping is stimulating and works on tissues, energy and your horse's attitude. Cup your relaxed hands into a roof shape and just clap them alternately up and down on muscle areas so that only the fingertips and heels of your hands make contact, creating a characteristic 'puffing' sound with each clap.

Rolling

Don't forget that rolling is nature's own physiotherapy and a horse's idea of ecstasy. Make opportunities for your horse to roll on a stone-free area as often as possible. If he is stabled, bring him out and let him roll in hand, keeping in front of his head with the leadrope loose, allowing him to roll from side to side; he will then get up and have a good shake. After work, remove his saddle and hold the reins as above, letting him roll – a perfect way to relax and dry off.

(The techniques shown in these photographs should only be attempted by a trained professional therapist.)

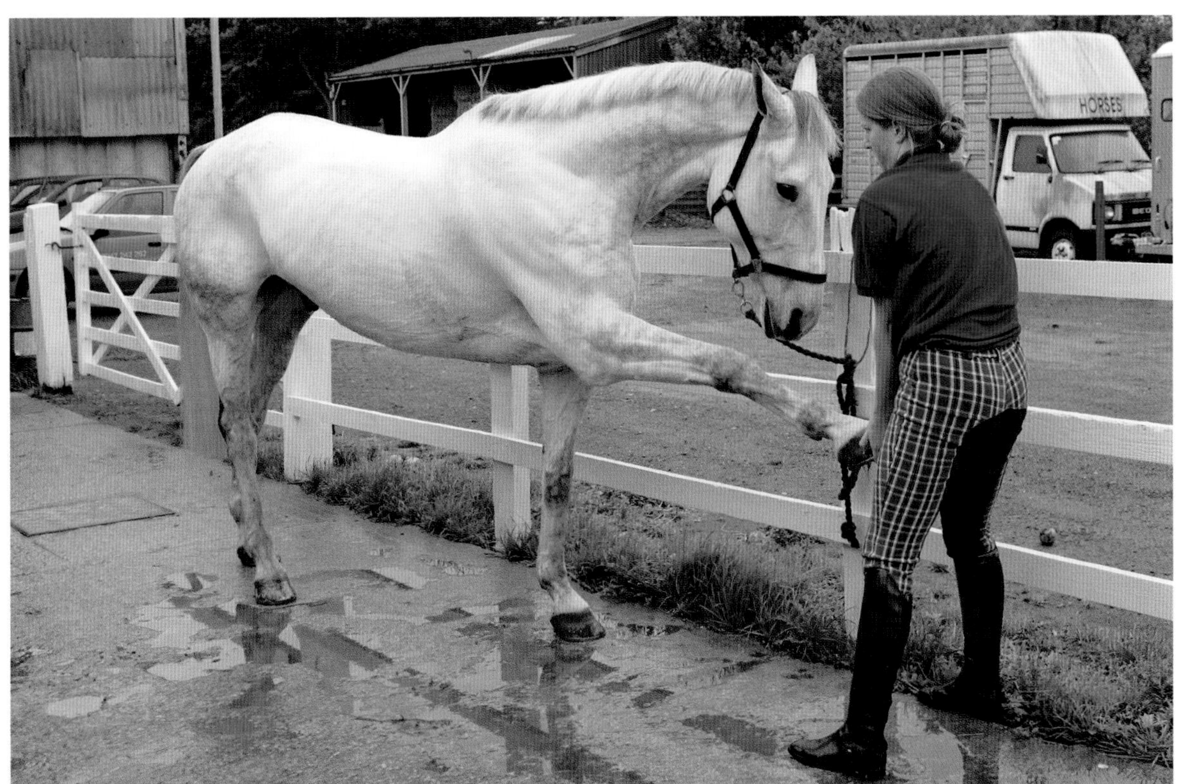

83 Consider learning to heal

By 'heal' I am referring to the natural healing abilities that most, or even all of us, have, although we may not realize it. Of course, there is a great deal of controversy about such things as hands-on healing, distant healing, Reiki, chakras, auras, energy, self-healing and similar ideas, and people of all denominations try to explain them, or explain them away, in terms of their own beliefs. Let's consider a few angles.

Belief versus knowledge

The two are not the same, but both are perfectly valid when it comes to healing. To *believe* something is to have firm faith or trust in it. To actually *know* something means to have categorical, undeniable proof of it, maybe due to scientific work or personal experience. Both can have profoundly positive – or negative – effects on the minds of animals or humans, so both are undeniably effective. How you use them, therefore, is of crucial importance to your horse.

Optimism

Animals and humans all have differing personalities and temperaments, but it must be said that the optimistic ones among us enjoy happier, more fulfilled and usually more successful lives (and not merely, or even actually, in material terms) than the pessimists or the realists. It pays in all ways to be an optimistic person, to avoid the negatives in life where possible, and to surround ourselves with uplifting, beneficial factors. This certainly influences our animals, and promotes good health and happiness all round. And often, of course, our animals perform this favour for *us*, don't they?

Down-to-earth love and care

Just knowing that you are loved and cared about, ideally in an unconditional way, has an enormously beneficial and healing effect. Merely emanating a truly caring attitude to your horse – handling him sensitively and confidently, and letting him know by your actions and daily routine that you are trustworthy, that his needs and wants are always catered for and that you have a caring, loving regard for him – is a form of healing because it reassures and calms him. And horses who enjoy a noticeable 'bond' with their owners also act as a healing force on *them*: it is a self-perpetuating double circle.

Being calm and feeling comfortable and safe produces 'good' chemicals and hormones in the body and mind that can actually heal (don't just believe it – know it!) and maintain good health. Being tense, worried, anxious or frightened produces 'bad' chemicals that can actually cause illness and lead it to continue, too: ask any doctor, veterinary surgeon or human or animal health professional. Those horses that live in a loving, caring environment are happier, and thus generally healthier, than those in a tense, uncaring environment in which their fright, flight or fight response is permanently switched on, albeit sometimes at a low level due to anxiety. Being in good, happy health also helps us fight back at life's inevitable traumas.

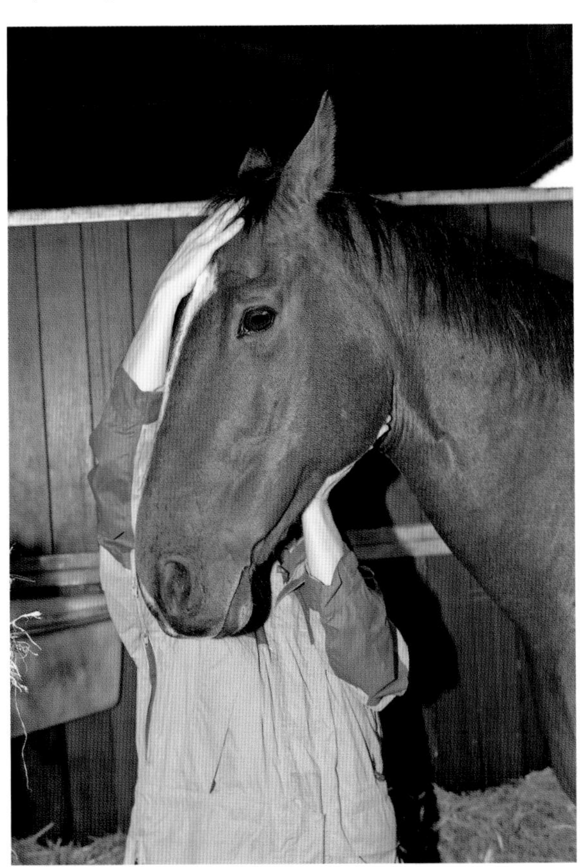

Try a bit of healing

I am a trained equine shiatsu therapist (shiatsu is a therapy related to acupuncture, and is known to be effective). It has created interest in several other modalities or forms of healing, and the following basic technique was given to me by a professional healer. I have found it genuinely helpful, and offer it to you to try – with an optimistic mind. You can use it in the presence of the person or animal, or distantly.

1. 'Ground' yourself by imagining that your feet are rooted in good, productive earth.
2. Protect yourself from 'bad energies' by surrounding yourself in your mind with a cloud or bubble of white light, white being said to be protective.
3. Picture or look at the object of your healing, and visualize them being surrounded by a cloud of healing (I use green, which is said to be a healing colour). You can put your hands lightly on or near them, if present, and visualize healing passing from your hands into their body – and you can do this to yourself, too. Imagine it soaking into their whole body and mind, especially any troublesome parts, and continue until you feel that you have sent out enough, for the time being.

Next day, observe your horse or lightly ask the person concerned how they feel, and I'll bet you get a genuinely positive response. Do this daily for them: I know it will help.

How about something more formal?

Would you like to train in some form of healing? There are many complementary therapies, and if you are reading this particular topic you may well already be drawn to a particular one, or more. (See page 151, in particular *Complementary Therapies for Horse and Rider*).

At this level, whether or not you accept money for your services, you will ultimately need professional indemnity insurance, and will probably need to be registered with an appropriate administering organization.

Remember – start your quest with an open, optimistic mind, and don't think, or let anyone tell you, that you are chasing rainbows. You're sure to find a therapy that is just 'you' – and everyone has to start somewhere. Experts weren't always so expert, and there's no reason why you shouldn't become one. If money to train is a problem, start by searching your local library for suitable books, get the free magazines from complementary health shops, read up on things, and take it from there.

84 Never let anyone bully your horse into transport

Loading horses into trailers or horseboxes seems to cause more trouble than any other single problem. It also seems to create a great deal of abuse, raised tempers in humans, fear and even terror in horses, unwanted advice from onlookers, some good and some bad, and general *Angst* all round. Various ways of overcoming the problem are offered, and if you have the facilities, there is one humane, proven cure.

The psychology of the situation

In days gone by the solution to anything a horse would not do was often to 'let him have it' – in other words, to beat him up until he did whatever it was. Unbelievably, this is still the attitude of many people, both when handling horses on the ground and when riding them.

Horsemen and women with a 'feel' for horses will be able to judge when a horse is genuinely frightened and when he is just being awkward – and despite the protestations of some people, this does happen with some individuals. A lot depends on the horse's temperament: some are genuinely difficult even from birth, some are amenable all their lives despite reasons to be otherwise, and some just need a bit of 'no-nonsense' cajoling.

It seems to be generally agreed by most 'thinking' horse people that beating a horse up or otherwise abusing him in a particular situation, such as loading into transport, will not only make him more reluctant to go in in the future, but will in fact also constitute cruelty. If you are planning to take your horse anywhere, make very sure that you and he are well practised in loading, travelling and unloading before the intended date, so that you are unlikely to be faced with a horse who won't load, or be desperate enough to allow someone else to try.

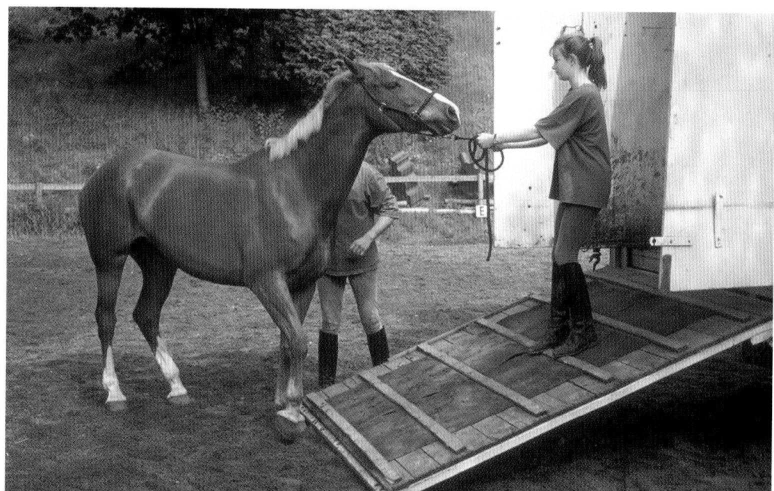

And what about the 'proven cure'?

Park your trailer or horsebox in the paddock with all the ramps down, and leave it there for a few days. Pad or otherwise guard sharp edges and corners. It often happens that the horses, curious creatures that they are, will investigate it, and will end up going in and out at will, sometimes using it for shelter.

If this does not happen, start leaving goodies at first near the ramp, then on it, then in the entrance, and then right inside so they have to go in. Also start feeding them inside, and you will probably find that this regime, which takes some days, will result in success, as it has for many people in the past.

85 Discover which colours your horse will walk on

Have you ever noticed that most trailer and horsebox ramps are covered in black rubber matting, and that many rubber and synthetic mats sold for use in stables are black, although some are green? It has been suggested that horses see black as a hole in the ground and are naturally reluctant to set foot on it, which could account in part for the apparently increasing number of horses who don't want to load into transport.

Red carpet treatment

A few years ago, an Equine Behaviour Forum member reported that her horse seemed frightened to enter his stable once black matting was put down on the floor. There was an area just inside the door with no bedding on it, and he seemed really scared of this. She discovered through trial and error that he would enter willingly if she put red carpet over the black matting, and gave the reason, as above, that she felt he feared that the black was a hole that had suddenly appeared at the entrance to his home.

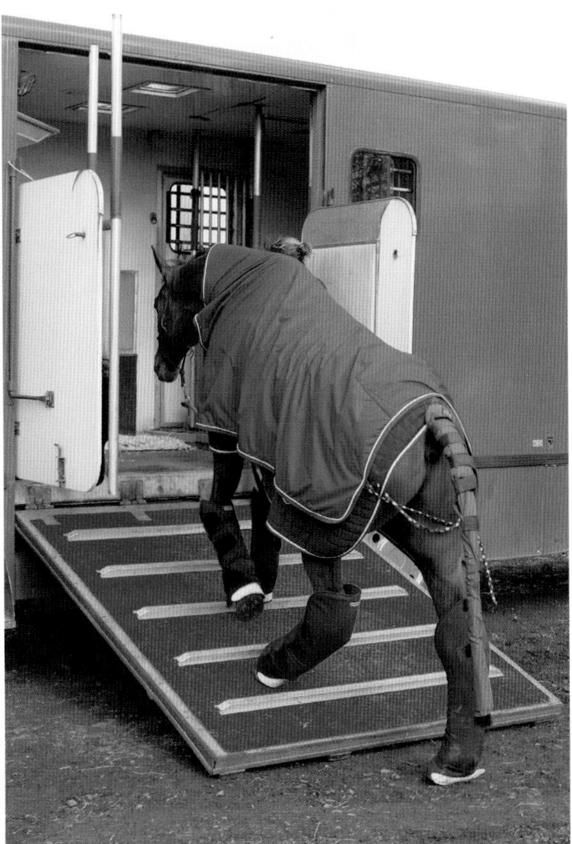

The idea was interesting enough for a college student to use it for her degree dissertation, and she also found that horses walked readily on red surfaces, and also, if I remember correctly, green colours – which is not surprising since the latter is the colour of grass.

Do your own trials

Whether or not you have problems in this area, it would be interesting and useful to know what colours your horse seems to find it safest to walk on. Presumably this would involve acquiring pieces of carpet or matting of different colours, and leading your horse over them. It seems that horses see reds and blues, but other colours less distinctly, so it would be a good plan to use red, orange, yellow, green, blue and violet – the whole of the spectrum that *we* can see – in order to arrive at a comparative result.

Apart from being interesting, this could be a key to a loading problem, and you might end up taking a roll of red carpet with you whenever you travel – probably to the amusement of any onlookers.

I should point out that different results arise in experiments, and much also depends on how light-reflective the colours are. For instance, some horses jump rustic, natural-coloured poles quite freely but baulk at coloured ones, whether or not they are shiny. However, horses being horses, those trained only over coloured fences often refuse rustic ones in the show ring, although they will jump them happily out hunting.

When you have found out what your horse is happy with, it would be helpful if you would send your conclusions to the Equine Behaviour Forum (see page 152).

86 Try to be present for treatments

At some time in their lives all horses will have to undergo various treatments, from the slightly worrying to the quite painful, and you can never be sure just how yours will react until he has experienced it. Sometimes you expect trouble and it does not arise; at other times a normally quite amenable horse will kick up a real fuss for no apparent reason. How your horse is handled on these occasions can improve or compromise his behaviour for a very long time.

Why might he be frightened?

All of us, animal or human, have a right to be at least concerned when something is being done to us that appears to be potentially painful or frightening. Whilst humans can have things explained to them (and don't professional health workers always play down the discomfort?), animals cannot.

The horse is a flight animal, and in general seems to have a fairly low pain threshold and also an excellent memory. So although a treatment may be tolerated innocently the first time, if it has hurt or frightened them, it will almost certainly cause trouble on the next occasion. This is the horse's survival mechanism working as it was designed to do so.

Associations

It is known that a horse can be distracted from a treatment by giving him food or a tasty titbit while it is going on, and this practice is very well worthwhile because it creates a good association. It is also important to choose very carefully, if at all possible, who is going to treat your horse, because you need to try to make the occasion as comfortable and uneventful as possible.

Personal, caring attention

If you have a good relationship with your horse, he is likely to behave better and feel safer with you in charge than with anyone else. I have known horses ruined for shoeing because the owner was not present and the yard proprietor left horses in the 'care' of a rough farrier. Mine was one of them, many years ago, and I never let it happen again.

Your horse will feel reassured by your presence – and those titbits – and although some things are inevitably unpleasant or painful, speak to the person concerned so they make every effort to minimize the discomfort as much as possible. You can play a great part in persuading the horse to put up with things by a calm, firm, sympathetic attitude, at the same time reassuring him and praising him when he co-operates. He will understand, and it will make everyone's life easier in future.

87 Learn your horse's vital signs

Strictly the term 'vital signs' is that given to the horse's temperature, pulse and respiration – the functions that are essential for life and are reliable signs of his state of health. Knowing the general vital signs of the horse species is very useful, but all individuals vary, and knowing your horse's fairly precise vital signs, and any deviation from them, can alert you to even the slightest and earliest signs of trouble.

Normal averages

The following are regarded as normal averages for the species at rest and not excited:

Temperature: about 38°C or 100.4°F for an average-sized riding horse.
Pulse: about 32 to 42 beats per minute (bpm)
Respiration: about 8 to 16 breaths per minute, in and out counting as one

Old horses have slightly lower readings than young ones, and fit ones have lower readings than unfit ones. Ponies have higher rates than horses because of body size.

To work out your own horse's individual averages, take his rates every day for a week in his stable or field when he is relaxed, resting and has not worked recently; this will give you a reliable idea of his normal at-rest rates.

How to take his rates

Temperature: The most accurate thermometers are proper veterinary ones available from your vet's practice. Shake the mercury well down below the figure for normal, with a snapping movement of your wrist, holding the thermometer at the opposite end to the bulb. Spit on the bulb to lubricate it. Stand behind and to the left of your horse, bringing his dock towards you with your left hand held over the top of it, which is a firm hold.

Gently insert the bulb into the anus with a gentle, side-to-side swivelling movement and push it in to about a finger's length, keeping firm hold of the end. Tilt it slightly so that it touches the wall of the rectum, and leave it in for the time stated on it. Gently pull it out, quickly wipe it clean, and read off the temperature.

Pulse: The most common place to find the pulse is inside the jawbone just down from the round part. Use your four fingertips in an even line and feel for the artery, which runs over the jawbone and feels like a springy cord. Using a watch with a second hand, count the beats for half a minute, then double your count to get his bpm.

Respiration: Stand behind and just to one side of your horse and watch his opposite flank rise and fall. You can also hold a mirror or piece of glass up to his nostril and count how often it mists up, or feel his breath on your hand. On a cold day, you can see the steam his breath creates.

88 Try to avoid livery-imposed changes

Livery yards vary widely in their quality: some are wonderful, whilst others can make life very upsetting and difficult for horses and owners alike. One infuriating situation is when your horse's stable is changed from one he likes to one he doesn't, to make way for someone else: this is upsetting for both the horse and his owner. So too is a change of grazing partners: losing his friends is bound to upset the horse.

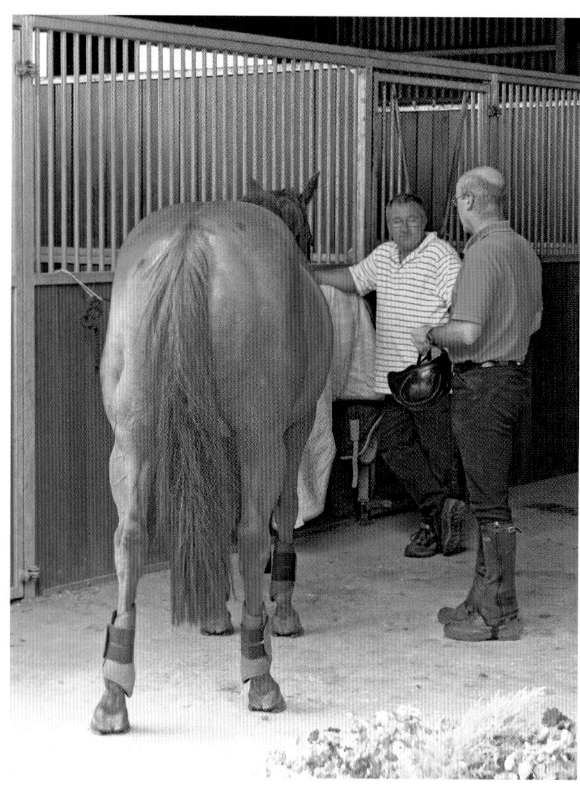

Two sides to every situation

To be fair, even the most accommodating yard proprietor can sometimes have an impossible task in keeping clients (owners) and consumers (horses) happy. It is good business to do this and to keep most boxes rented all the time (although an isolation box or two may be needed). Equally it can be difficult for some proprietors to turn down a new client because the only box he or she likes is already rented by a good client with a much-valued horse.

From your own viewpoint, as client, once your horse is happily settled in his box, with his friends and in a secure routine, you don't want to upset him and disrupt his life just because someone else wants your box. But on the other hand, if your horse does not particularly like his box, or you are fairly sure he would be better off in another one – bigger, better ventilated, lighter, next to his friend, for instance – being asked to move may create an opportunity for improvement.

The worst scenario is when you are simply told that your horse is moving, or even has been moved, because his box is wanted for some other horse belonging to a new or even existing client or for the proprietor's own horse, or his grazing partners have been changed because a new horse has arrived.

What can I do?

The best way of guarding against this sort of thing is to have a clause inserted in your livery contract (which all good yards will provide) confirming that this will not happen without your willing consent. If the proprietor will not agree to this, or inserts a coverall clause giving him or her *carte blanche* to do whatever they wish regardless of other clauses in the contract, you have no security at all over your horse's living conditions.

This is not good for your horse's psychological stability, maybe other people's horses, your own peace of mind or the proprietor's reputation and business. You could try to reason with the proprietor, stressing the above, but if this does not work, be prepared to move to a better yard if necessary. Always keep a list of other possible yards so that you are not left with nowhere to go. Such a change could be less disruptive to your horse in the long run.

89 Husband/partner out and horse in?

The idea of swopping your partner and your horse can have its attractions, depending on the state of your relationship, of course. Your horse may not really appreciate being brought into your house, and only your partner will know whether or not he would mind being kicked out. The point is, how do you choose between the two?

There's just something about horses ...

It seems to me after various experiences of relationships, both my own and the observed ones of other people, that horses are even more important to women than cars are to men. In the horse world at least, the old saying that women live for men but men live for their cars (or their work) does not seem to apply.

There are still women who mainly stay with their men because these husbands/partners make it possible for them to have their horses (and there are still plenty of those): these same women say that if the place were on fire they would save their horse first. Some readily admit that if their 'other half' demanded they choose between him or the horse, the horse would win outright. When a UK horse magazine ran a survey on this very topic some years ago, I seem to remember that it was over 80 per cent of (female) readers who said they would choose their horse over their man.

But I ask you, what sort of a man would give his beloved that sort of ultimatum? If the lady had her horse before this relationship started, then the horse is part of what she is, of what she does and what he fell for – but so many men seem to think that once the relationship seems safe he can set about changing her and introduce a few non-negotiable, surprise conditions. Big mistake!

What can I do?

The best way round this dilemma is to accept that life is all about compromise, on both sides, and to come to some agreement whereby both partners get *mostly* what they want (being intelligent, reasonable adults) but the horse gets *everything* he wants (it's not fair to make him suffer just because your other half is feeling jealous). After all, it's your relationship we're talking about here – your relationship with your horse, that is.

And if you really do want the 'ideal equine partnership', there really is no contest...

Not breaking the bond

Keeping the relationship strong

There are all sorts of ways in which we can, quite unintentionally, destroy our relationship with our horses. We may not even realize that it is happening until we have a feeling that we aren't getting on quite as well as we used to, that the horse seems a little more distant or on edge, or that our channels of communication aren't as open as before. At this point, less sensitive riders will start to look to the horse rather than themselves for the reason for the problem. They may assume that he is becoming too 'familiar' with them, 'trying it on' (a very popular phrase), 'wanting too much of his own way' or 'getting lazy'.

Horses are flesh and blood like us, and are not all angels – but few of them are downright skivers. I am sure that most of their quirks and 'difficult behaviour' arise out of self-defence. I feel they do understand what we called in the Eighties and Nineties the 'work ethic': they understand a job of work, and many of them like having a job because it makes them feel part of the human-horse herd. Many who are left out of things or see their owners dealing with another horse, make their disappointment known unmistakably.

If something starts going even slightly wrong in the relationship between a horse and his owner, we should always look to ourselves first. Ultimately it may be found that there is something wrong with the horse – something physical, or some sub-clinical (virtually unnoticeable) disease that affects his well-being.

The golden key

The most important single principle is *never to take your horse for granted.*

- Don't assume that he will always be there for you, forgiving, loyal and caring in his own way. Horses are not boot-lickers like most dogs (and I hate to say this, because I adore dogs): dogs are the quintessential unconditional lovers, but horses are not. They are excellent judges of people and situations, and they treat them according to how they assess them. They remember good and bad treatment, and you have to earn their acceptance and their forgiveness.
- Keep 'talking' to each other. Pay attention to him and see if he is trying to tell you something in some way. Keep your mind open and relaxed for this to happen. Talk meaningfully and clearly to him quietly and occasionally, and look for a response.
- Always treat him as special, and he will treat you the same way. Maybe you are the only person he greets without putting his ears back. Doesn't that make you feel special? When you are at the yard, he will show his bond with you by watching where you go all the time, by coming over to you and leaving his friends, by taking an interest in the things you are doing to him, and guarding your safety when you are out together. A partnership like this is truly worth cherishing.

90 Don't break the trust

There is an old saying in show business that you are only as good as your last performance, and this could easily be applied to your relationship with your horse. You are only as good a partner as was indicated by your behaviour at your last meeting. This is because horses remember infallibly what you do to them, and if you did something objectionable they will remember it, even if they don't act on it – yet.

Natural psychologists

Some horses are specific in their attitude to humans, treating different people differently and always appropriately. If you want to know what kind of horse person someone is, watch the horses they deal with, and these will tell you plainly by their demeanour and attitude. Other horses have a blanket view of humans, not liking any of us, or treating us all with interest, respect and even apparent affection.

Being able to categorize fellow herd members is an integral part of horses finding their place, and their friends, in the herd hierarchy. This is important enough in the wild, but in a herd of horses in a livery yard it can be even more crucial because of the frequently changing population. This skill is transferred readily to their relationships with humans: they quickly learn who they can trust to treat them well, and who they can be fairly sure will cause them anxiety.

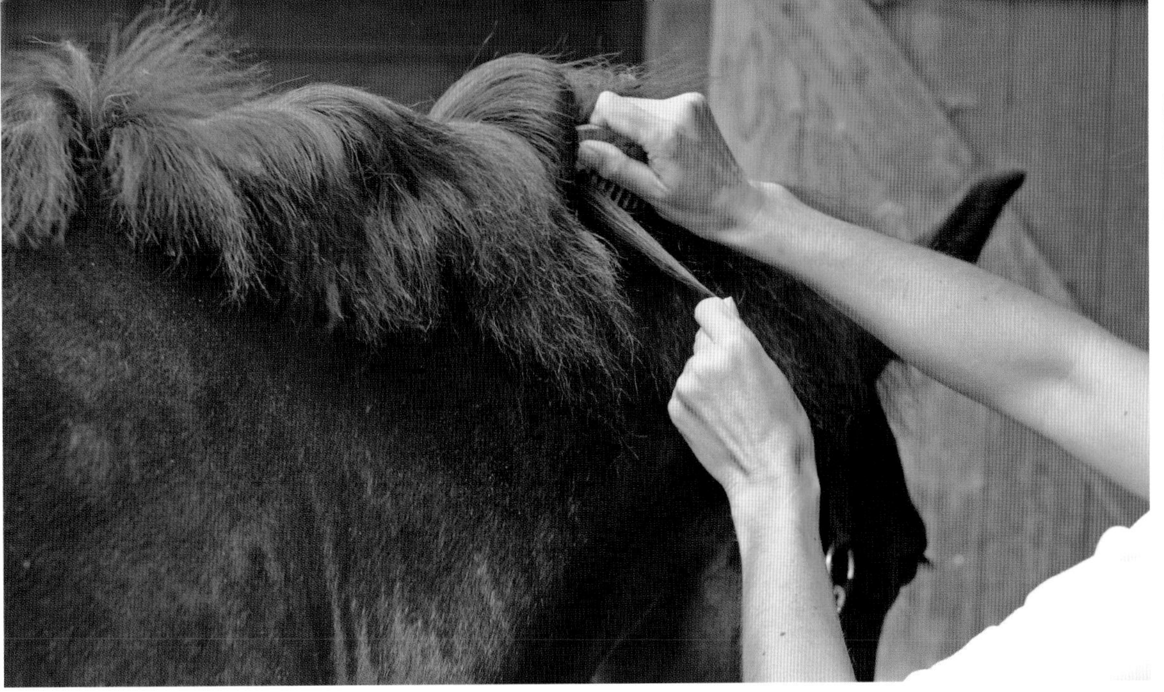

On having trust

Trust means having faith and confidence in someone to behave in a certain way. You can trust a thief to steal things, so you keep your treasured items out of reach. You can trust a well-mannered horse to not bite or kick you, so you may walk around him feeling quite safe. A horse trusts us to be the sort of person he perceives us to be from his own experience of us.

In what ways do horses trust us? They can certainly trust us to not hurt them. This is fairly basic and easy to understand. If we once hurt them, perhaps by accidentally knocking a bony part of their body with a bucket or rake, pinching their skin or taking their breath away when we girth them up, they will remember it. They may not take any action the first time, but if someone does something similar and it starts to make them wary of having humans in their stable, we can rightly say that they have lost trust in us. This might relate to just one particular aspect of a horse's management, such as a bridle put on carelessly, or it might be to having someone in his box at all because he is expecting them to do something unpleasant to him.

Horses trust us and expect us to be consistent. They will treat us according to their current view of us whether that is good or bad, but we normally use the word 'trust' in a positive, rather than a negative sense. The title of this topic is 'Don't break the trust', and that clearly means trust in a positive way.

Under saddle, trust is very easily lost by means of harsh riding methods that are often centred on the mouth because many people seem to have no idea of what a genuinely sympathetic contact is. Indeed, I find when teaching that a strong and fairly rigid contact has often actually been taught by a previous instructor as correct, which it is not. When out riding, we can also drop down in our horse's estimation by trying to force ('discipline') him to go somewhere he is clearly afraid of. Handling such a situation badly with force instead of firm, kind patience can break the trust between you very quickly.

What can I do?

Because trust is clearly so fragile, yet so essential to a close relationship, make sure, as far as you can, that you preserve it. If you often make life unpleasant, uncomfortable, painful or frightening for your horse, there is no way he is going to trust you. Many are easily upset and frightened, and although they may put up with a lot, that doesn't mean that they trust us or regard us as valued partners.

Trust can be broken in the following ways:

- Making your horse associate you with pain and discomfort, such as putting on tack or rugs that do not fit.
- Handling him without care for his comfort, such as bridling less than carefully and not making sure the bridle and bit are comfortable; also snatching the bit out of his mouth and banging it on his teeth when unbridling, instead of allowing him to let go of the bit slowly, in his own time.
- Riding in a saddle that does not fit.
- Scrubbing at sensitive areas with the dandy brush, or using the metal curry comb on him.
- Subjecting him to the discomfort of having his mane and tail pulled the old-fashioned, traditional way when there is now equipment that enables you to do both jobs humanely if you really need to.
- Nicking his skin when clipping him.
- Allowing gates and doors to bang shut on him.

Basically, treat your horse as you would wish to be treated yourself if you were in his place.

91 Provide leadership or support

There is still disagreement as to whether or not horse and pony communities recognize leaders in the way we do. They clearly recognize support and discipline from birth, because a foal's first experience of a relationship is with his dam. He receives protection and discipline from her from the outset, so he learns early about leadership and support – but does any other horse take her place later?

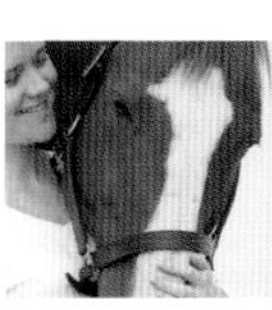

Both sides of the argument

There are opposing schools of thought on this subject. Some people believe that horses do not operate in terms of leaders and followers – that is, having a herd boss, or even bosses over different aspects of herd life, whom others normally obey. They maintain that horses basically want a peaceful, quiet life (true), and prefer to function on the basis of mutual friendships with 'preferred associates' rather than according to the more usual mammalian hierarchical society. It certainly seems to be this way when you observe a stable, well-balanced herd of domestic or feral horses or ponies – although if they are all contentedly observing their places, there will not be any trouble, anyway.

Members of a different school of thought believe that horses do definitely have some kind of hierarchy in their herds, and claim, logically enough, that if they did not, they would be the only mammals without a culture of leader, perhaps occasional assistants and followers. It certainly seems to be this way, too, when you observe other herds that are not so stable, with comers and goers who, even though familiar, upset the current status quo of who is grazing with who, who is sheltering where, and so on. The arrival in the field of a particular horse can quickly make it obvious, even if only temporarily, as to who gets his way and who doesn't as the herd reorders itself.

Another type of herd consists of the truly floating population, such as at a dealer's yard, a training centre where horses come and go for schooling, and livery yards that can't keep their customers: in these, the likelihood of leaders and followers becomes more probable as horses frequently chivvy around for a slot in the herd – there are always some horses who nobody argues with, and some who are regularly kicked about.

What about horse-human relationships?

So do horses recognize leaders, or at least superiors and inferiors? I belong to the school that believes they do, both in their own herds and in their relationships with humans. It is certainly the case that when a human tries to operate with a horse on the basis of equal friendship, it never works. The horse takes over if he feels superior to the human or is a 'leader' type; and if he isn't, he becomes as boring and socially unacceptable as an undisciplined human teenager who cannot cope with freedom.

From a safety viewpoint, horses are not equipped to make decisions in human society. They can have no concept of how badly they can hurt both themselves and us if they do not do as we ask them. Even a simple request such as moving laterally to the right (so that we can miss that drain with no grating on top) can be fatal if the horse refuses, because he might get a leg down the hole, break it and have to be destroyed. We might fall off during the same incident into the path of a vehicle, and could be injured or even killed.

Not providing leadership or support (both terms being used rather loosely) is bad for horses living in human society, as nearly all do, because I am sure that, deep down, most horses function more contentedly if they co-operate with a firm, strong and fair human who calls the shots, treats them well, meets their needs, does interesting things with them and is reliably consistent.

You have a much better chance of building up your ideal equine partnership with a horse living in those circumstances than with one who feels adrift and insecure because he cannot cope with a life without a foundation of confidence, reliability, security and, therefore, safety. He will have no kind of respect for you, either the kind we recognize or whatever kind horses recognize.

What can I do?

Always remember to be calm, firm and positive with your horse:

- **Calmness** is catching, and allows information to reach your horse's brain and mind.

- **Firmness** instils confidence in you and self-confidence in the horse that, in our terms, you will make the right decisions for both of you.

- **Being positive** (in other words, being upbeat and decisive) instils a feeling of safety and trust.

Take the trouble to learn as much as you can about all aspects of horses so that you can handle, manage, train and ride or drive your horse correctly, appropriately for him and with confidence, which he will certainly sense. Be open-minded enough to continue learning and to seek professional advice when you feel you need guidance.

All the time you are dealing with your horse, have in your mind the attitude that he is the most important thing in your life (even if he isn't quite), that you want the best for him, that he is safe with you, and that you want both of you to be happy. These sorts of thoughts get through just as effectively as more negative ones, and affect, even determine, your partnership.

92 Don't leave your horse without supplies

Equines in wild or feral conditions are almost never hungry because their food is all around them. It takes a drought to significantly reduce the growth of their food or the availability of their water supply, even if they have to trek to it. What does all this mean in relation to our domestic horses? It means that being hungry is unnatural for horses: they are not adapted to it, and it can cause digestive disorders and psychological distress.

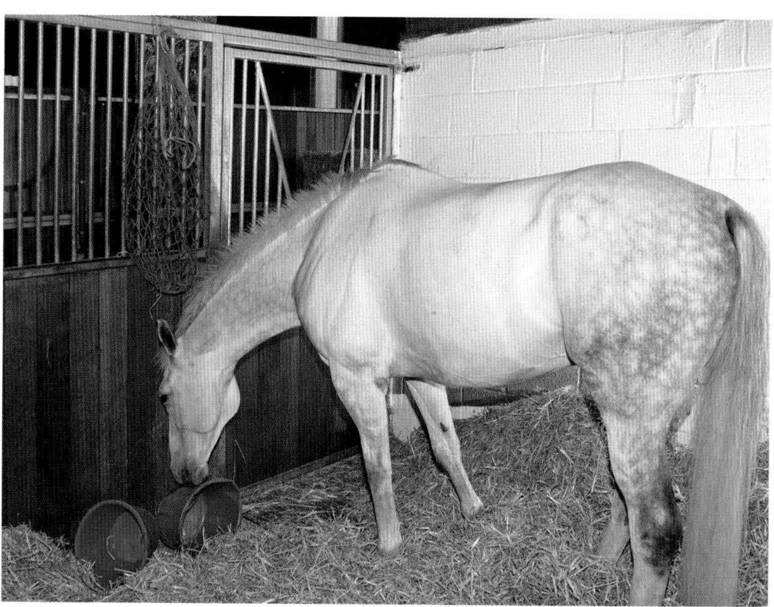

How does this affect my relationship with my horse?

If you are your horse's main or only carer, he knows very well that it is you who will normally give him his food and water. Many horses are quite capable of asking for, or actually demanding, refills of hay and water when they need them. They also know very well the usual times when feed is brought round on their yard and when they are turned out to graze. Even on do-it-yourself yards where there is no real routine, most owners turn up at similar times each day, and horses get used to this.

Although it is hard to state this categorically, I think it is quite likely that when your horse becomes hungry or thirsty because he has no hay left and no drinkable water, he thinks about you because you are associated with attending to his needs – and those thoughts are coupled with anxiety, hunger, thirst, insecurity and some degree of psychological suffering and physical discomfort.

This is certainly not the way to form a close partnership with your horse based on trust, confidence in you and contentment.

Many owners skip out, feed, hay up and water their horses before going to work for the day, say at around 7.30am. But by midday the hay will probably have gone, and so might the water, or it could be tainted and undrinkable. In reality, the horse has no supplies at all, and will not get any until the owner returns at about 6pm – and not even then if he/she is going to ride. This is a very common situation, and it is made even worse for the horse when he knows others are being fed and watered.

What can I do?

Either try to get to the yard at lunch-time, or arrange for someone else to hay up and water your horse, and preferably skip out and also adjust his rug, if he wears one. And if you are going to ride in the evening, try to arrange for someone to give him a small feed at about 4pm. This won't take long, and it will make all the difference to your horse's state of mind and body.

If this isn't possible, leave your horse double supplies of hay and water on any occasion when you know you are not going to visit him again for several hours.

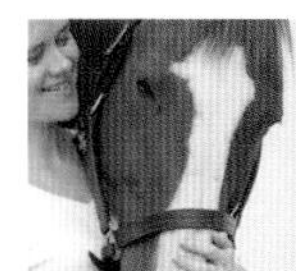

93 Don't leave your horse out in bad conditions

Horses vary in their responses to, and views of the weather. A few graze in pouring rain with impunity, some don't bother too much about wind, and a few lucky ones don't seem to attract many troublesome insects. Others, though, are badly affected by all these, and one weather element that all horses seem to hate is being out for long in relentless, hot sun. Just because a horse is out, it doesn't mean he is happy.

'Natural' horse management

Keeping a horse out in bad conditions is a very common practice, not only among some 'natural' horse keepers who, in their sometimes unconsidered zeal, take things to the extreme. Although most of us want our horse to go out for grass, freedom and play with others, there are times when it would perhaps be better to leave him in and either exercise him ourselves, or turn him out for shorter periods. The combined system of horse keeping (partly in, partly out) has many good things going for it.

Horses cared for by mainly one person will associate that person with their quality of life and show very clear relief when he or she arrives to rescue them from rough outdoor conditions. Unfortunately, perhaps they also associate that owner with having put them there in the first place, but we'll never be certain.

What constitutes rough outdoor conditions?

Rough and unsuitable outdoor conditions include:

- Squelching, sodden ground with little or no grass and no alternative forage.
- Hard, baked, cracked or stony ground with, again, little or no grass and no alternative forage.
- A field with no area flat and comfortable enough for horses to lie and rest if left out for long periods.
- No drinkable water (filthy, slimy troughs or stagnant ponds), or a water supply with an off-putting approach such as rubble to 'prevent poaching', a steep-sided pond or knee-deep mud.
- No effective shelter: this usually means providing an approachable, welcoming man-made shelter unless the field is, unusually, well serviced by thick hedges all round and a dense tree canopy overhead. Even these, however, can seethe with flies in summer and drip with rain during a prolonged spell of wet weather.
- The presence of a domineering, aggressive or troublesome bully who has decided that your horse, or one of his friends, will be his victim.
- Being made to wear for many hours an ill-fitting or unsuitable rug (too hot/skimpy) and/or headcollar that is uncomfortable and may even be causing pain.

What can I do?

Think very carefully about the conditions your horse's turnout area offers, and consider what you can do to improve matters, if at all possible, by avoiding the sort of conditions described above. If you can't, consider an alternative area and management regime for your horse, which caters for his needs and his comfort.

94 Don't leave a horse stabled with no company or attention

Horses kept in conventional stables are undeniably deprived, to a greater or lesser extent, of some of their basic needs, depending on the design of the stable. Many cannot touch or smell each other, both of which are important social needs, and can only see other horses stabled nearby or walking past without any contact. These conditions are outdated, horse-unfriendly and can encourage distress and stereotypies or 'stable vices'.

It can get worse!

Stables of the design described above were the product of man's imagination, not horses' needs. They were devised to prevent horses supposedly bickering with each other, to the extent that their resting and eating patterns were disrupted and they felt threatened if they were the one inferior in status. These situations are not completely prevented, though, if two unfriendly horses in this type of stabling are housed next to each other (which is bad management anyway), because each knows that the other is on the other side of the wall, so there is still a measure of unease.

Stabling of this design is bad enough on its own, but the horse's lot is made worse when he is the only one left in the yard and receives no attention for several hours. There are very few horses who will not be unhappy and stressed by mistreatment of this sort.

Again, your horse looks to you to create his security, contentment and safety, and a horse living a life of low quality must associate it with his carers.

What can I do?

If, for some reason, your horse has to be left in alone when others are away or out, try your best to arrange for a friendly horse or pony to be in with him, either in his stable if they are friends and it is large enough, or next door or free in the yard outside so they can talk over the door and yours does, at least, know that another horse or pony is close by.

If the situation arises often, you may need to review your management policies, as this is a very unsuitable and unkind way in which to keep a social animal such as a horse.

It can be a big help if you and a friend keep your horses on the same yard and treat them more or less as a social unit, so they can be turned out together even if no other horse is, or left stabled together when necessary. This completely solves the above problems; in addition, you can both share your chores and arrange your timetables to ensure adequate attention for both horses.

95 Don't leave your horse alone in the field

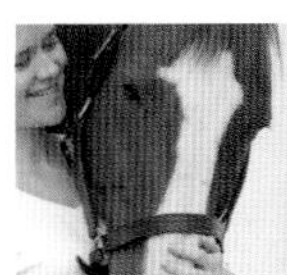

There are very few horses or ponies who are altogether happy left alone in a field for many hours, or even for just half an hour in some cases, even when there is plenty of grass, water and shelter. Some will tolerate it quietly, and sometimes it is useful to be able to turn a horse out on its own rather than not at all; but it is not what most of them really want. Even if a companion horse is not a close friend, its presence is reassuring.

Won't the horse be too busy eating to care?

Possibly some will, but *most* won't. If a horse is used to being turned out for a short time alone, for instance whilst his owner does the chores and prepares his stable ready for his return, he gets used to this routine and will probably have a graze and a play. The problems start when he is left out for several hours, his initial hunger for grass is satisfied, he has played and rolled to his heart's content, the sun gets up, and the flies and midges become a torture to him and he can't escape them; furthermore he has no equine friend for moral support and there is no sign of his owner coming to save him.

In winter, other problems arise. Grass is normally very unappetizing at that time of year, and the ground is often muddy, which brings its own problems in the form of softened, sometimes even rotted feet, thrush from long exposure to wet conditions (it is not just dirty bedding that causes it) and mud fever (scratches in the USA). New Zealand rugs can become extremely uncomfortable after just a few hours if they slip round, pull, dig in or leak; and if a strap or surcingle breaks they can slip right out of position, which can be positively dangerous. Again, lack of company increases your horse's feelings of insecurity and anxiety.

All this, of course, affects your horse's quality of life and creates very definite feelings of general anxiety, insecurity and discontent, and can also lead to poor physical and mental health, which often accompanies a life of distress and neglect.

What can I do?

- Don't think that because your horse is out he will be fine on his own because he will graze (unless you know him really well and can say, in all honesty, that he doesn't mind).
- If he has to be out for a short period alone, try to put him in a field next to others with a really good dividing fence or hedge between them, just in case.
- When conditions are bad at any time of the year, make other arrangements to ensure that he is sheltered, comfortable and provided for, and that he has the support of a friend.

96 Don't reprimand your horse unjustly

There are many trainers and behavioural practitioners who believe and advise that horses should not be reprimanded at all, just praised or rewarded when they do something right. However, there are just as many who believe, like me, that correction administered at minimal levels and in a way the horse understands, as happens in a herd, is essential to his confidence and the safe performance of his job.

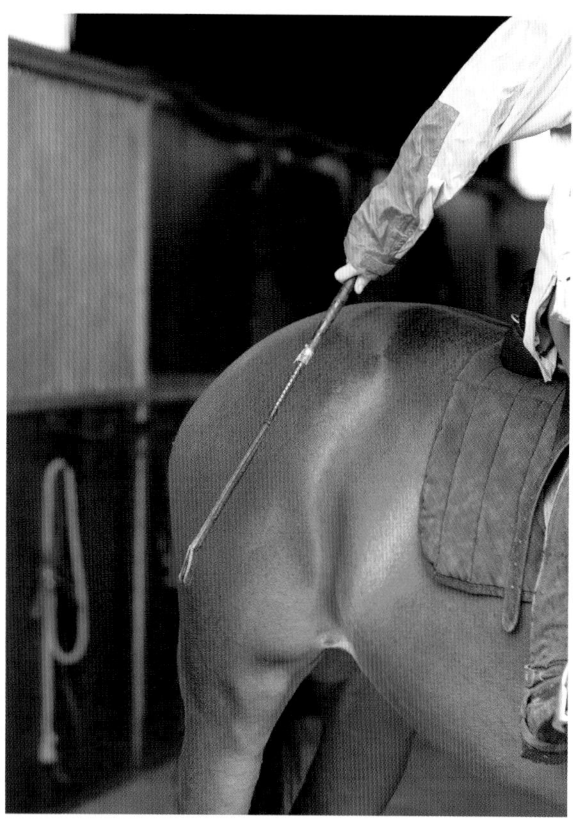

The horses' way

Like most people and animals, horses prefer to spend their time doing just what they want. Unfortunately, this is rarely possible, either for them or for us, and right from the start young horses are shown what is acceptable in horse society and what is not.

They are not simply rewarded when they get something right and ignored when they do something wrong. In practice, their 'reward' or 'praise' when they do something acceptable or welcome – such as mutual grooming, offering friendship or joining in flicking flies away from others' faces with their tails – is acceptance in the herd or by a particular individual. When they do something unacceptable, such as harassing another horse or trying to mate with a mare, they most certainly are not ignored but are corrected by means of short, sharp, shock treatment – for instance being kicked or bitten – or something longer term, such as being driven off, at least temporarily.

As they grow up they try to push out their boundaries, particularly males who will want to form their own herds one day and may need to fight another for the prestigious job of herd stallion. They get plenty of experience of what is acceptable to the herd stallion and the mares, and what is not.

The humans' way

When handling, schooling or training a horse we use a short, sharp reprimand or correction, such as a firm 'no', a growl (very effective, I find) or one slap of a whip, if we are certain that a horse knows he is really behaving unacceptably. Many people, however, often go disastrously wrong in the following ways:

- They fail to make the correction instant, which is crucial to the horse's understanding of it. The horse will only understand that he has done something unacceptable to us if he experiences something unpleasant – a correction – at the same time or within a second or two at the most of its happening. The logic is, in our terms, that he thinks 'I won't do that again because this will happen as well.'
- They make the punishment too strong, often far too strong, for the 'crime'. This sort of thing usually consists of thrashing with a whip, which, to make matters even worse, is often applied several seconds after the horse has done wrong or even not done right. This is not correction or reprimand: it is brutal abuse.

Reprimanding a horse unjustly means doing it when he does not understand the reason (usually because we have done it too late), or when he is incapable of complying because of pain, fear, or lack of fitness or athleticism. Nothing is more guaranteed to wreck your relationship than abusing and confusing your horse.

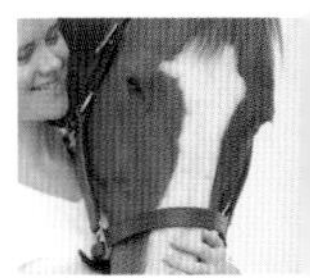

It can take very astute judgement to be certain why a horse is not complying or is 'misbehaving'. This is one reason why only praising horses and not reprimanding them can be excellent advice for those who are not skilled enough to make that decision: it is better by far than reprimanding unjustly and incorrectly.

Correcting or reprimanding a horse does not mean that he is treated unnecessarily harshly. It can be as mild as the word 'no' spoken in a normal tone of voice, if this is familiar and he knows, from past experience, that what he has just done is unacceptable in this human-led herd.

Teaching a horse 'no' as a correction/reprimand is as useful and important as teaching him 'yes' or 'good boy' as praise/reward. Dr Marthe Kiley-Worthington, in one of her books (see page 151), makes the point that many people are very quick to correct a horse when he does 'wrong' but are very slow to praise him when he does right, if in fact they praise him at all.

Praise and reward, too, must be given extremely quickly if the horse is to be sure he has got something right; again, he has to associate it with his action or it is wasted and can even be confusing.

What can I do?

If you feel that you cannot tell for certain whether or not your horse is apparently misbehaving or not doing what you ask because he is being 'difficult', is in discomfort or pain or just does not understand, do not reprimand him. Use the principle of just praising and rewarding him (making life pleasant) the instant he does something right, or stops doing something wrong.

If you are skilled enough to be certain of the situation, reprimand him just by using the word 'no' spoken sternly, or give a growl, then as soon as the horse stops doing the wrong thing or does the right thing, praise/reward him instantly.

Remember that 'instantly' means just that, or two seconds after at the most – no later.

97 Don't allow 'rough riders' to ride your horse

Most owners allow other people to ride their horses at some time, but it pays to be careful whom you allow to do so. If a horse has a bad experience with another rider, this can colour his view not only of that person but also the place or circumstances in which the unpleasantness occurred, no matter who is riding him, including his owner. If you are present during the experience, who knows what thoughts will be in his head?

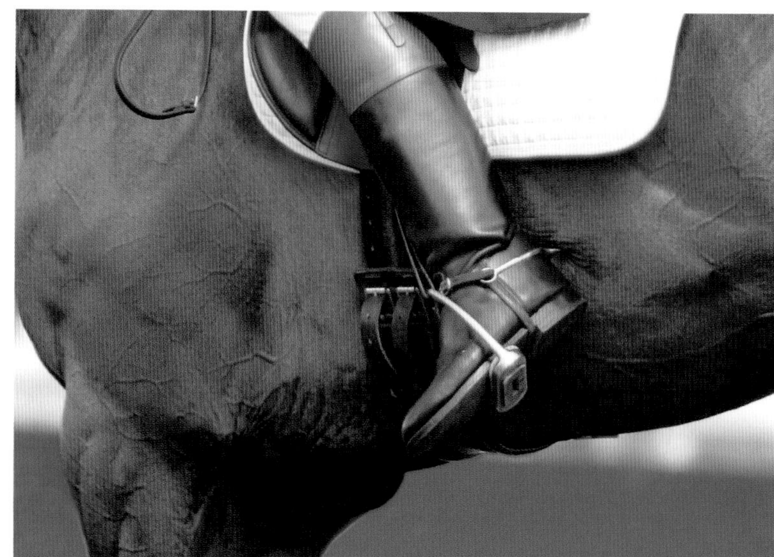

The trouble with saying 'yes'

The matter of allowing someone else to ride your horse can be quite tricky. Those who ask to ride him are likely to be friends, close acquaintances or instructors or trainers. With a friend, either you know them well enough to tell them that they are simply not a good enough rider, or you may know that if you refuse they will be offended – and so you agree to their riding him, albeit against your better judgement.

With acquaintances, it is an easy matter for you to say that you very rarely allow people to ride him, as you don't want him to be confused by techniques that are different from yours, whatever these are.

The problem may come when your instructor expects to ride the horse and, once he or she is on top, you may see that their style of riding is harsh and your horse is distressed. Unfortunately, this is quite a common situation. I have ridden, schooled and taught people on horses who have been beaten up by instructors, had their mouths ruined, their sides injured by spurs, their minds thoroughly mixed up, and whose confidence has been well and truly shattered.

If anything like this happens in your presence it may upset your horse, depending on his temperament, for quite some time afterwards, and it does nothing for his trust in you. It can undo months of good work you have done with him, distress him and leave you feeling guilty for having allowed it.

What can I do?

You can simply make it a firm rule that no one, but no one, ever rides your horse but you, or only a very few carefully selected riders, because too many simply confuse him. You don't have to apologize when saying this. If you come across someone whom you feel would really benefit your horse by riding him, or at least would do no harm, and it is convenient or helpful to you for them to ride him, you are perfectly entitled to make an exception. However, do all you can to watch them ride another horse first, if at all possible, to see if you think they would get on with yours.

98 Do not fail to insist on good behaviour

Horses are obviously flesh-and-blood creatures with minds of their own. Some appear to be very quick learners, whether they learn from us, or from their own experiments and experiences. They are certainly quick to assess us and know whether or not we are safe to have around, whether they should be wary of us and whether we are strong and reliable or weak and inconsistent.

On knowing where he stands

We have already talked about how horses behave with each other, either in a feral herd or in domestic circumstances, and have concluded that, although horses may have no actual sense of right and wrong, they definitely learn what is acceptable and what is not. We have to admit that they are fairly simple-minded creatures, and once they have learnt something they rely on it as a sort of rule of living. Therefore if they are going to feel confident in you, and safe in your presence and when doing the things you ask of them, they need to know from one moment to the next how you behave and how you react to them.

If you don't stick to your principles and insist that your horse sticks to them too, he will never be sure what is acceptable behaviour and what is not, because he cannot rely on you and the code of behaviour you expect from him. This is very unsettling for a horse and makes him feel insecure – which is obviously not the way to forge an ideal partnership.

If you fail to insist on good behaviour – good stable and field manners, and safe behaviour under saddle – you will very probably end up with a horse who pushes you around and thinks nothing of it. If you then reprimand him he will be confused because he is only behaving in the way you have accepted from him before: you cannot insist on good behaviour one minute and then let him behave like a moron the next if you want him to feel safe in your company and look to you for the good things in his life.

What can I do?

Just be consistent in expecting good behaviour from your horse. If his weak point, say, is refusing to stand still when being groomed, you can just tie him up, of course, but it would be more beneficial if you insisted every single time that he stand in a certain place as you groom him, and every time he moves a foot, put him back, without fail.

If you cannot be bothered to correct him for a misdemeanour on any one occasion, then he will do it again and again in the future. He needs to be in the habit of co-operating with you, and he never will if you are not consistent. He will also not respect or feel safe with what he sees as an unreliable person.

99 Don't work your horse in a forceful way

Everyone in the horse world knows, or knows of, people who are hard on their horses. The well-worn phrase 'show the horse who's boss' has become synonymous with harsh, even brutal treatment, and with an attitude of regarding the horse as more or less guilty before he has even done anything. Forceful, coercive methods that are stressful on the body and distressing to the mind are the norm for many people.

The crux of the matter

The main cause of all this is the attitude of *some* people towards horses, and maybe animals in general. Many owners feel that their horse is inferior to them and must be domineered, allowed no initiative, go in a prescribed way for as long as the rider demands, and accept without argument tack and equipment that ultimately causes pain because of pressure or the artificial way in which it forces the horse to go. Argument, indeed, invites abuse in many horse-human relationships: reins, nosebands and gadgets are yanked tighter, whips and spurs are used harshly, bits are hoisted higher and mouths are abused pitifully. Horses cannot possibly feel emotionally close to people with whom they associate this kind of persecution.

It is particularly worrying when this mistreatment is advised ('ordered') by instructors, and the owner often carries it out because 'my instructor told me to do it' as if they cannot identify harsh treatment when they see it.

- First of all, the instructor has no business to tell a client to abuse their horse or to abuse the horse themselves, and if they cannot see that it is abuse they have no business to be training horses or teaching people.
- Secondly, the owner who cannot see and feel that it is abuse has no business to work a horse until they have learned to think for themselves and have developed more knowledge of and empathy for horses in general.

What constitutes bullying and abuse?

Dictionary definitions of 'abuse' and 'bully' are:

abuse To make bad use of, ill-treat, attack, revile, cause suffering.

bully One who uses strength or power to hurt or intimidate others; blusterer, tyrant, persecutor, oppressor, coward, torturer, hired ruffian.

Let us now examine some methods of riding, schooling and working, which thoughtful people may probably regard as abusive and bullying.

Working a horse when he is not sound or physically comfortable. The horse must have no problems at all with his body that will cause him discomfort or pain when worked, whether from the ground or the saddle.

Working a horse when he is not fit to do the work demanded. Schooling can be hard work, and although it will, itself, promote athletic fitness, strength and suppleness, these must be built up gradually. A great deal can be achieved in walk and short spells of trot until the horse adapts.

Forcing horses with training aids into a required outline. Some training aids are very helpful as long as they are adjusted so that they only come into effect when the horse is working incorrectly, so that they suggest, rather than force him into a more beneficial posture.

Working the horse for extended periods in a forced 'outline'. Very short stints of schooling, up to about three minutes or less depending on fitness, enhance physical development and psychological willingness and co-operation. Then the horse needs a break on a completely loose rein.

Harsh use of bits, whip and spurs. In general, horses should be schooled to be sensitive and co-operative enough to go from the seat (weight) and mind, with legs and hands used tactfully in support. Yanking the horse's mouth, spurring him hard and beating him up, all of which some riders do regularly, constitute abuse in anyone's book. (Effective, humane techniques are covered in more detail in *100 Ways To Improve Your Riding* and *100 Ways To Improve Your Horse's Schooling* – *see page 151.*)

Riding with a hard contact, virtually holding his head in place. We must always ride 'from back to front', allowing with the reins to tactfully show the horse where he should place his head in order to acquire a beneficial and safe weight-carrying posture of the whole body.

Working or riding in equipment that is wrongly adjusted. This includes things such as high bits, tight nosebands, tight saddles, saddles placed too far forwards that restrict the shoulders, girths that dig in behind the elbows when the horse tries to move freely, and draw-reins, running reins, side-reins or any other training device that is adjusted too tightly.

Say 'no' to all this

I want to suggest that all owners think hard about more humane ways of riding their horses, and resolve to say a firm 'no' to any trainer who recommends bullying, abusive and harsh methods. Truly kind, knowledgeable and effective horsemen and women have shown for generations that these methods are not necessary, nor are they a part of good horsemanship. Don't accept them from others, and don't use them yourself, no matter who tells you to do so, if you want a close, rewarding partnership with your horse.

100 Don't just be a horse user: be a horse lover

The horse has always been mainly a working animal ever since it was domesticated. Some are kept for breeding and seem to have an easy life, but horse breeding the human way can be very distressing to horses. Keeping horses simply to use them in some way, whether for breeding, food or working, will always go on, but it could be carried out more humanely, and it is, of course, no way to form a relationship or partnership with a horse.

Why own a horse?

People don't own horses for no reason at all. We all know why we have horses, and I suggest that the very best reason to own a horse is because you want one, because you love horses enough to commit your time, spirit and money to creating a partnership with a horse, because you like horses' company and are probably drawn to them in a way that many of us are familiar with but cannot explain.

Other reasons for owning horses are to compete against other horses and riders; to have a goal or aim (good performance); to be part of a club or team; to receive prizes, adulation and compliments; for self-achievement; as a means of exercise and company with another creature, because you like looking at them in your paddocks; and various other reasons. All these reasons are absolutely fine, *provided* the horse's welfare and well-being comes before anything else he can do for you.

This is not an unrealistic statement: I simply do not believe that animals are here for us to use as we wish. If we are taking something from an animal, we should definitely make sure we do it humanely and kindly, particularly in view of the fact that the horse probably does not have a choice in the matter. True, horses are quite capable of objecting if we do something appalling to them – although many don't. They are capable of kicking up a fuss, depending on their temperaments, if we make what they feel are unreasonable demands, and they can refuse to do certain things.

We're in charge

Basically, though, we control their lives, and if we don't get on with a horse it is the horse who is moved on, not the human. The horse has no say in where he goes, or what someone else may try to do with him. In truth, our society *does* 'use' horses – of course it does – but I feel that provided we put the horse's welfare first, this is fine. Many horses love working, love being part of the active life of a busy or a quiet yard, love and need to feel valued and wanted. This is how their minds evolved. Lone horses are often miserable and in the wild would be in great danger, and in my experience 'used' horses, as opposed to loved ones, are also miserable.

Individual relationships

Horses are very sensitive and know full well when they are not cared about. They may not have any concept of being actually used, but they do know when they are not cared about or loved. Just as we can feel when someone appears to like or dislike us, or simply feels completely indifferent towards us, so can horses, I am sure. Again, as with people, sometimes we find that either we can understand and get on with a particular horse almost instantly, or we cannot.

It is often revealed in biographies and autobiographies, articles, interviews and the like, how close some top riders, competitive or otherwise, are to their horses or to horses allocated to them. In *My Horses, My Teachers*, the late Col. Alois Podjahsky of the Spanish Riding School gives many anecdotes about individual horses who taught him whilst he was supposedly teaching them, and how he was drawn to some and had problems with others.

Of course, having problems with a horse does not mean that you do not love him, are not putting him first or, indeed, don't get on with him. The most challenging relationships often work out to be the strongest and best once you have both learned to understand and live with, or work with, each other. Some only come to fruition because the rider did not have the attitude of *using* his or her horse, but because they wanted the best, the perfect outcome, for that horse and their hoped-for partnership. The fact that they ultimately achieved top honours in their establishment, won gold medals, championships or taught hundreds of beginner or nervous riders to have confidence in them and relate to a horse was not the owner's top priority. Perhaps if the horse had not felt good about his owner and his life, he would never have been able to do his job so well. I know that this regularly happens. Horses diminish in spirit when they are not appreciated for themselves, but they blossom and thrive when they are.

Horse users do not appreciate their horses for themselves, only for what they can do, and do for them. Horse lovers appreciate their horses for themselves and treat what they can do for them as a bonus, as the icing on a delicious cake – a cake that is addictive in the best possible way.

Conclusion

So what is the ideal partnership?

I suggest that the ideal partnership between horse and owner is one that is synergistic – where one plus one equals four – or rather, one in which you both feel content and fulfilled when you are together, one in which each is concerned when there is something wrong with the other and acts accordingly as best he or she can. In short, the ideal partnership is one in which you each come before anything else in your horse life.

If you 'must' go to a competition and you take your horse to it despite knowing he is not on good form, whether this is for your own sake or for fear of not letting down a team, the horse will be troubled or may lose confidence or faith in you, and whatever partnership you were forming is at least put on the back burner.

People who have a horse because they want something to dominate, want some means of showing how powerful they are because they can control and manipulate a big, strong animal like a horse, or show how competent they are because they can bend it to their will, are not even in the running for a true partnership. People who want to, as they see it, earn kudos in their milieu of associates, or even make up for some inner sense of insecurity shown by an excessive desire to '*achieve*', do not even have a partnership on their horizon.

The kind of people worth impressing are not those who think along those lines. If you must seek the approval of other people, as far as horses are concerned, seek to be known for your kind and effective 'way' with them, for how your horse has improved in spirit and well-being since he came to you, for giving good and appropriate help and advice when people come to you for help, and for doing what you can to lessen mistreatment of horses by your example, advice and actions. If you know deep down that you should report a particular case of abuse or cruelty to a horse to an appropriate authority, then *do it*.

To finish, I should like to refer readers back to the very start of this book, to the Five Freedoms (see pages 4–5]. These cover every practical point concerning the care of horses. Horses kept according to these principles will be well cared for, but that extra dimension that comes with the ideal partnership between a human and a horse, which may come because of that, is something that only you and your horse can feel. Other people can spot it in you and can help you to achieve it, but only *you* know the nature of it, and only the two of you can let it happen.

Acknowledgements

My sincere thanks go to all The Team at David & Charles for their usual professionalism and patience during the creation of this book. Writing books is always very much a joint effort which is not often realised by the reading public, and their creative and technical input is always invaluable.

Just as much patience and expertise is required by the photographer/s and so I want to let David and Sally Waters of Horsepix know just how much I appreciate everything they have done, often above and beyond the call of duty, to provide most of the images for this book.

The human and equine models for most of the pictures demonstrated, posed and set the scenes generously and, I hope, not without enjoyment and some challenge. I am most grateful to them all, in particular for their being willing to demonstrate the wrong ways to do things as well as the right ways.

Further reading

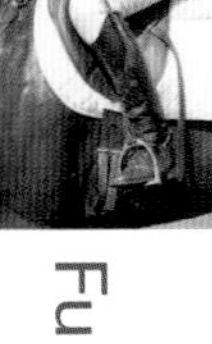

Other books in the *100 Ways* series by Susan McBane and published by David & Charles:

100 Ways To Improve Your Riding (2004)
100 Ways To Improve Your Horse's Health (2005)
100 Ways To Improve Your Horse's Behaviour (2005)
100 Ways To Improve Your Horse's Schooling (2006)

Bishop, Ruth, *The Horse Nutrition Bible* (David & Charles, 2003)
Bromiley, Mary W., *Massage Techniques for Horse and Rider* (Crowood Press, 2002)
Budiansky, Stephen, *The Nature of Horses* (Weidenfeld & Nicholson, 1997)
Clemence Mews, Anna, and Dicker, Julie, *What Horses Say – How to Hear, Help and Heal Them* (Kenilworth Press, 2004)
Hannay, Pamela, *Shiatsu Therapy for Horses* (J. A. Allen, 2002)
Hogg, Abigail, *The Horse Behaviour Handbook* (David & Charles, 2003)
Kiley-Worthington, Marthe, *Equine Education* (Whittet Books, 2005)
Kiley-Worthington, Marthe, *Horse Watch: What It Is to Be Equine* (J. A. Allen, 2005) and any other books by this author
Lijsen, H.J., and Stanier, Sylvia, *Classical Circus Equitation* (J. A. Allen, 1993)
Loch, Sylvia, *Invisible Riding* (D. J. Murphy, 2005) and any other books by this author
McBane, Susan, *The Horse Owner's Essential Survival Guide* (David & Charles, 2005)
McBane, Susan, *Bodywork for Horses* (Sportsman's Press, 2005)
McBane, Susan, and Davis, Caroline, *Complementary Therapies for Horse and Rider* (David & Charles, 2001)
McBane, Susan, *How Your Horse Works* (David & Charles, 1999)
McGreevy, Paul, *Equine Behavior: A Guide for Veterinarians and Equine Scientists* (Saunders, 2004)
McLean, Andrew, *The Truth About Horses* (David & Charles, 2003)
Peace, Michael, *The 100% Horse* (David & Charles, 2006)
Podhajsky, Alois, *The Complete Training of Horse and Rider (as Carried Out at the Spanish Riding School)*, (various editions)
Skipper, Lesley, *Let Horses Be Horses* (J. A. Allen, 2006) and any other books by this author
Stanier, Sylvia, *The Art of Lungeing* (J. A. Allen,1993)
Stanier, Sylvia, *The Art of Long Reining* (J. A. Allen,1995)
Stanier, Sylvia, *The Art of Schooling for Dressage* (Sportsman's Press, 2005)
Swift, Sally, *Centered Riding* (J. A. Allen, 2006)
Swift, Sally, *Centered Riding 2* (J. A. Allen, 2002)
Williams, Moyra, *Understanding Nervousness in Horse and Rider* (J. A. Allen, 1990 and 1999)
Wilson, Anne, *Top Horse Training Methods Explored* (David & Charles, 2004)
Wood, Perry, *Real Riding* (Kenilworth Press, 2002)

Useful addresses

The Association of British Riding Schools
Queen's Chambers
38–40 Queen Street
Penzance
Cornwall TR18 4BH
Tel: 01736 369440

Association of Riding Establishments of Northern Ireland
126 Monlough Road
Saintfield
Co Down BT24 7EU
Tel: 028 9751 0381

The British Equestrian Trade Association
Stockeld Park
Wetherby
N. Yorks., LS22 4AW
Tel: 01937 582111

The British Horse Society
Stoneleigh Deer Park
Kenilworth
Warwickshire CV8 2XZ
Tel: 01926 707700

The Classical Riding Club
Eden Hall
Kelso
Roxburghshire
Scotland TD5 7QD
Fax: 01890 830667
www.classicalriding.co.uk

The Equestrian Book Society (book club)
Brunel House
Forde Close
Newton Abbot
Devon TQ12 4PU
Tel: 01626 323200

The Equine Behaviour Forum
Flat 2
169 Sumatra Road
West Hampstead
London NW6 1PE
(Please enclose s.a.e.)
www.gla.ac.uk/external/EBF

The Equine Shiatsu Association
St Peter's Stud
Church Lane
Upper Beeding
West Sussex BN44 3HP
Tel: 01903 814860

The Equine Sports Massage Association
17 Gloucester Road
Stratton
Cirencester GL7 2LB
Tel: 01285 650275

Farriers Registration Council
Sefton House
Adam Court
Newark Road
Peterborough
Cambs. PE1 5PP
Tel: 01733 319911

W. H. Giddens
now incorporated into
Schnieder Riding Boots
16 Clifford Street
London W1S 3RG
Tel: 0207 734 0433

Intelligent Horsemanship
Lethornes
Lambourn
Berkshire RG17 8QS
Tel: 01488 71300
www.intelligenthorsemanship.co.uk

Society of Master Saddlers
Kettles Farm
Mickfield
Stowmarket
Suffolk
Tel: 01449 711642

TTEAM – Tellington Touch Equine Awareness Method
TTEAM Centre
Tilley Farm
Timsbury Road
Farmborough
Bath BA2 0AB
Tel: 01761 471128
www.ttouchtteam.co.uk

Index